What People Are Saying about Threshold Bible Study

"This remarkable series provides a method of study and reflection that is bound to produce rich fruit." ▨ **DIANNE BERGANT, C.S.A.**, *Catholic Theological Union, Chicago*

"This fine series will provide needed tools that can deepen your understanding of Scripture, but most importantly it can deepen your faith." ▨ **MOST REVEREND CHARLES J. CHAPUT, O.F.M. CAP.**, *Archbishop of Philadelphia*

"*Threshold Bible Study* is a wonderful series that helps modern people read the Bible with insight and joy." ▨ **RICHARD J. CLIFFORD, S.J.**, *Boston College School of Theology and Ministry*

"This is a wonderful gift for those wishing to make a home for the Word in their hearts." ▨ **CAROL J. DEMPSEY, OP**, *University of Portland, OR*

"Written in a sprightly easy-to-understand style, these volumes will engage the mind, heart, and spirit." ▨ **ALEXANDER A. DI LELLA, O.F.M.**, *The Catholic University of America*

"By covering a wide variety of themes and topics, *Threshold Bible Study* continually breathes new life into ancient texts." ▨ **JOHN R. DONAHUE, S.J.**, *St. Mary's Seminary and University*

"*Threshold Bible Study* offers a marvelous new approach for individuals and groups to study themes in our rich biblical and theological tradition." ▨ **JOHN ENDRES, S.J.**, *Jesuit School of Theology, Berkeley*

"*Threshold Bible Study* offers you an encounter with the Word that will make your heart come alive." ▨ **TIM GRAY**, *President of the Augustine Institute, Denver*

"*Threshold Bible Study* offers solid scholarship and spiritual depth." ▨ **SCOTT HAHN**, *Franciscan University of Steubenville*

GOD'S SPOUSAL LOVE

THRESHOLD
BIBLE STUDY

GOD'S
SPOUSAL
LOVE

Stephen J. Binz

TWENTY-THIRD
PUBLICATIONS
twentythirdpublications.com

TWENTY-THIRD PUBLICATIONS
A division of Bayard
One Montauk Avenue, Suite 200
New London, CT 06320
(860) 437-3012 or (800) 321-0411
www.twentythirdpublications.com

ISBN: 978-1-62785-266-1
Library of Congress Control Number: 2017936956
Printed in the U.S.A.

Contents

How to Use
Threshold Bible Study

E ach book in the Threshold Bible Study series is designed to lead you
through a new doorway of biblical awareness, to accompany you
across a unique threshold of understanding. The characters, places,
and images that you encounter in each of these topical studies will help you
explore fresh dimensions of your faith and discover richer insights for your
spiritual life.

Threshold Bible Study covers biblical themes in depth in a short amount
of time. Unlike more traditional Bible studies that treat a biblical book or
series of books, Threshold Bible Study aims to address specific topics within
the entire Bible. The goal is not for you to comprehend everything about each
passage, but rather for you to understand what a variety of passages from different books of the Bible reveals about the topic of each study.

Threshold Bible Study offers you an opportunity to explore the entire
Bible from the viewpoint of a variety of different themes. The commentary
that follows each biblical passage launches your reflection about that passage
and helps you begin to see its significance within the context of your contemporary experience. The questions following the commentary challenge you
to understand the passage more fully and apply it to your own life. The prayer
starter helps conclude your study by integrating learning into your relationship with God.

These studies are designed for maximum flexibility. Each study is presented in a workbook format, with sections for reading, reflecting, writing,
discussing, and praying. Space for writing after each question is ideal for personal study and allows group members to prepare in advance for their discus-

sion. The thirty lessons in each topic may be used by an individual over the period of a month, or by a group for six sessions, with lessons to be studied each week before the next group meeting. These studies are ideal for Bible study groups, small Christian communities, adult faith formation, student groups, Sunday school, neighborhood groups, and family reading, as well as for individual learning.

The method of Threshold Bible Study is rooted in the classical tradition of *lectio divina*, an ancient yet contemporary means for reading the Scriptures reflectively and prayerfully. Reading and interpreting the text (*lectio*) is followed by reflective meditation on its message (*meditatio*). This reading and reflecting flows into prayer from the heart (*oratio* and *contemplatio*).

This ancient method assures us that Bible study is a matter of both the mind and the heart. It is not just an intellectual exercise to learn more and be able to discuss the Bible with others. It is, more importantly, a transforming experience. Reflecting on God's word, guided by the Holy Spirit, illumines the mind with wisdom and stirs the heart with zeal.

Following the personal Bible study, Threshold Bible Study offers a method for extending *lectio divina* into a weekly conversation with a small group. This communal experience will allow participants to enhance their appreciation of the message and build up a spiritual community (*collatio*). The end result will be to increase not only individual faith but also faithful witness in the context of daily life (*operatio*).

Through the spiritual disciplines of Scripture reading, study, reflection, conversation, and prayer, you will experience God's grace more abundantly as your life is rooted more deeply in Christ. The risen Jesus said: "Listen! I am standing at the door, knocking; if you hear my voice and open the door, I will come in to you and eat with you, and you with me" (Rev 3:20). Listen to the Word of God, open the door, and cross the threshold to an unimaginable dwelling with God!

SUGGESTIONS FOR INDIVIDUAL STUDY

- Make your Bible reading a time of prayer. Ask for God's guidance as you read the Scriptures.

- Try to study daily, or as often as possible according to the circumstances of your life.

- Read the Bible passage carefully, trying to understand both its meaning and its personal application as you read. Some persons find it helpful to read the passage aloud.

- Read the passage in another Bible translation. Each version adds to your understanding of the original text.

- Allow the commentary to help you comprehend and apply the scriptural text. The commentary is only a beginning, not the last word, on the meaning of the passage.

- After reflecting on each question, write out your responses. The very act of writing will help you clarify your thoughts, bring new insights, and amplify your understanding.

- As you reflect on your answers, think about how you can live God's word in the context of your daily life.

- Conclude each daily lesson by reading the prayer and continuing with your own prayer from the heart.

- Make sure your reflections and prayers are matters of both the mind and the heart. A true encounter with God's word is always a transforming experience.

- Choose a word or a phrase from the lesson to carry with you throughout the day as a reminder of your encounter with God's life-changing word.

- Share your learning experience with at least one other person whom you trust for additional insights and affirmation. The ideal way to share learning is in a small group that meets regularly.

SUGGESTIONS FOR GROUP STUDY

- Meet regularly; weekly is ideal. Try to be on time and make attendance a high priority for the sake of the group. The average group meets for about an hour.

- Open each session with a prepared prayer, a song, or a reflection. Find some appropriate way to bring the group from the workaday world into a sacred time of graced sharing.

- If you have not been together before, name tags are very helpful as a group begins to become acquainted with the other group members.

- Spend the first session getting acquainted with one another, reading the Introduction aloud, and discussing the questions that follow.

- Appoint a group facilitator to provide guidance to the discussion. The role of facilitator may rotate among members each week. The facilitator simply keeps the discussion on track; each person shares responsibility for the group. There is no need for the facilitator to be a trained teacher.

- Try to study the six lessons on your own during the week. When you have done your own reflection and written your own answers, you will be better prepared to discuss the six scriptural lessons with the group. If you have not had an opportunity to study the passages during the week, meet with the group anyway to share support and insights.

- Participate in the discussion as much as you are able, offering your thoughts, insights, feelings, and decisions. You learn by sharing with others the fruits of your study.

- Be careful not to dominate the discussion. It is important that everyone in the group be offered an equal opportunity to share the results of their work. Try to link what you say to the comments of others so that the group remains on the topic.

- When discussing your own personal thoughts or feelings, use "I" language. Be as personal and honest as appropriate and be very cautious about giving advice to others.

- Listen attentively to the other members of the group so as to learn from their insights. The words of the Bible affect each person in a different way, so a group provides a wealth of understanding for each member.

- Don't fear silence. Silence in a group is as important as silence in personal study. It allows individuals time to listen to the voice of God's Spirit and the opportunity to form their thoughts before they speak.

- Solicit several responses for each question. The thoughts of different people will build on the answers of others and will lead to deeper insights for all.

- Don't fear controversy. Differences of opinions are a sign of a healthy and honest group. If you cannot resolve an issue, continue on, agreeing to disagree. There is probably some truth in each viewpoint.

- Discuss the questions that seem most important for the group. There is no need to cover all the questions in the group session.

- Realize that some questions about the Bible cannot be resolved, even by experts. Don't get stuck on some issue for which there are no clear answers.

- Whatever is said in the group is said in confidence and should be regarded as such.

- Pray as a group in whatever way feels comfortable. Pray for the members of your group throughout the week.

Schedule for Group Study

SESSION 1: INTRODUCTION   DATE: _____

SESSION 2: LESSONS 1–6   DATE: _____

SESSION 3: LESSONS 7–12   DATE: _____

SESSION 4: LESSONS 13–18   DATE: _____

SESSION 5: LESSONS 19–24   DATE: _____

SESSION 6: LESSONS 25–30   DATE: _____

Thus says the Lord: I remember the devotion of your youth,
your love as a bride, how you followed me in the wilderness,
in a land not sown. JER 2:2

God's Spousal Love

Because spousal love is the most intimate and sacrificial love known to human beings in the natural world, the biblical authors fill the pages of the Bible with its narrative and emotional power. Countless stories of human love, engagement and marriage, anticipation and passion, pregnancy and birth, and infidelity and divorce fill the biblical literature. In fact, all of the Bible's sacred history can be described as an unending love story, as the inspired writers use the images and vocabulary of marital love to express the love between God and God's people.

The first chapters and the final chapters of the Bible—from Genesis to Revelation—form the bookends of the Bible, both of which offer images of spousal love. The first verses of Genesis begin with the expression of God's love through the act of creation, coming to its summit in the making of man and woman, the fullest image of God in the world. The narrative in the garden expresses the origins of spousal love through the story of woman being made from the side of the man. When she is presented to the man, he exclaims with joy that she is "bone of my bones and flesh of my flesh." This longing of spouses for one another becomes a symbol of God's desire for the intimacy of an everlasting marital covenant with humankind.

The Bible's closing scenes culminate in images of a great wedding, the marriage banquet of the Lord. The bride of Christ is presented as adorned for her husband. The longing of the glorified church for her risen Lord is expressed in the heartfelt cry, "Come, Lord Jesus!" The scenes anticipate the climax of the divine love story, the eternal unity of Christ and worshiping humanity. This is the joyful eternity anticipated and experienced sacramentally in the eucharistic liturgy of the church.

In between these opening and closing texts of the Bible we find countless expressions of divine spousal love. From the Torah, prophets, psalms, and wisdom writings of Israel to the gospels, letters, and apocalyptic literature of the church, the Scriptures present us with beautiful images of the Creator's love for humanity, the Lord's love for Israel, and Christ's love for his church. God and his people are bound by ties of the heart, and they mutually long for the eternal fulfillment of their deepest longings.

Reflection and discussion

- In what sense is spousal love the richest expression of human love?

- What other types of human relationships can image God's love for humanity?

Israel's Love Story with God

The heart-stirring narrative running throughout the Bible is tied together for us when we understand God's ultimate passion. Our God is an ageless lover who desires nothing more than to unite humanity with himself in a spousal covenant.

This divine desire begins to be expressed as God forms a bond of "steadfast love and faithfulness" with the Israelites. This covenant that God desires is so committed, so personal, so self-giving and life-giving that it can only be described in human language as a courtship, betrothal, and marriage. God enters this spousal covenant first with Israel, so that they might be an example to the surrounding nations of what it means to share in a committed covenant with God.

Israel's prophets communicate God's steadfast love as well as Israel's infidelity to the covenant through the language of spousal love. God is the husband who passionately loves his wife and who suffers deeply when his love is scorned. Israel is not grateful for the gifts that her divine husband has lavished upon her, so God takes them back and chastises her. But God's purpose is only to bring about repentance, reconciliation, and a renewed union.

During the time of Israel's exile, the prophets looked back to the exodus as the time when Israel followed God with bridal devotion and to Mount Sinai as the place where the marriage covenant was formed with Israel. Following Israel's adulterous behavior of following other gods and breaking the covenant, her divine husband does not repudiate her, but calls her to return to him. He promises to entice Israel back to the wilderness and then, in the days to come, to establish a new and everlasting covenant with her. The unfaithful wife will be welcomed back and the joys of love renewed forever.

The Song of Songs, a lyrical masterpiece about the joys of human love, was reinterpreted in Israel based on the prophetic words of spousal love. The Song came to express God's passionate love for Israel and the divine nuptial. It conveys all the freshness and joy of the couple in the garden of Eden. Paradise lost will become paradise regained and perfected without end.

As the prophets anticipate the future messianic age, they join the spousal imagery with the familiar biblical stories of the sterile wife who bore children through God's intervention. Jerusalem, who has become barren through conquest and exile, will have more children than she can hold. The once-abandoned city now includes the nations of the world in God's family. Far exceeding any previous expectations, God's people will include the whole of redeemed humanity.

God's spousal love always elicits hope for a continually better future. With undying love, God invites his people to receive a new heart, a new spirit, and a new covenant so that they can share a full-hearted bond with God and become the new creation God desires for humanity. God's steadfast love and faithfulness is without end.

Reflection and discussion

• What qualities of God's love are emphasized by the spousal imagery of the Old Testament?

• How does imagining the covenant as God's courtship, betrothal, and marriage enhance my understanding of the Bible?

The Wedding Feast of God's Kingdom Arrives

In the gospels, Jesus describes his ministry as a joyful wedding festival with himself as the bridegroom. When he is asked why his disciples do not fast, he replies that the wedding guests cannot mourn while the bridegroom is with them. Jesus uses the imagery again as he compares God's kingdom to a marriage banquet that a king makes for the marriage of his son. In this parable, Jesus again presents himself as the bridegroom and the kingdom as a wedding feast.

In John's gospel, John the Baptist is presented as the best man of the wedding, the friend of the bridegroom. The best man in the Jewish wedding prepares the wedding and conducts the bridegroom to the bride. According to the Jewish rabbis, Moses had this role in the spousal union of God and Israel. In the period of the church, Paul claims the role of the best man. He tells his Corinthian community, "I promised you in marriage to one husband, to present you as a chaste virgin to Christ." As the best man, Paul has the responsibility of preparing the bride and presenting her to the bridegroom.

Paul's most essential development of the marriage symbolism is found in his letter to the Ephesians. He urges spouses toward the kind of love by which Christ loves the church.

> Husbands, love your wives, just as Christ loved the church and gave himself up for her, in order to make her holy by cleansing her with the washing of water by the word, so as to present the church to himself in splendor, without a spot or wrinkle or anything of the kind—yes, so that she may be holy and without blemish. (Eph 5:25–27)

Christ's love is selfless and self-sacrificial. The ritual bath, made on the morning of the Jewish wedding, prepares the bride before she is clothed in bridal garments. Christ himself prepares the church because the bridegroom wishes to carry in his arms a beautiful bride. She is transformed by God's word and clothed in splendid garments, without wrinkle or stain. Paul brings together the principal matrimonial themes of Scripture: the gifts of the husband, the anticipation of the wedding, the beauty of the bride and her garments, and the mutual love of the spouses.

Paul describes Christ's love for the church as "a great mystery" to which Christian marriage must look as its model (Eph 5:32). Spousal love is an outward sign of the invisible mystery of Christ's love for his bride and his bride's love for him. This great mystery rules out any kind of domination or chauvinism in marriage. Rather, it points spouses in the direction of the cross. The grace of Christian marriage is a fruit of Christ's cross. He laid down his life for his church in order to save her and to be united with her. In return, she gives herself back to him as a spouse in response to his love.

For this reason and with this grace, spouses willingly share the sufferings of life out of love, in good times and in bad, in sickness and in health, for richer or for poorer, for as long as they both shall live. And in the joy of their love and family life, spouses in this life experience a foretaste of the eternal wedding feast of God's kingdom.

Reflection and discussion

- In what sense is the ministry of Jesus a joyful wedding festival?

- How do the spousal images of the New Testament enhance my understanding of Jesus and his church?

Spousal Love Reflects the Love of God into the World

The spousal language that permeates the Bible assures us that we are God's beloved. We are the spouse who calls to Christ, "Come, Lord Jesus," to make our life complete. We are not servants or slaves; we are beloved. We do not serve him out of a sense of fear, duty, or guilt. What spouse wishes to be loved by one who is motivated by intimidation or obligation? We are beloved.

We can take the matrimonial language of Scripture and apply it to our own individual relationship with God. We can recognize our own experiences in those of Israel: in her marriage covenant, then as unfaithful, punished, repentant, purified, pardoned, and called again to union with the bridegroom. We can see ourselves with Christ in the position of the bride, loved though undeserving, redeemed, and called to happiness in mutual love.

Christianity's mystical tradition has applied these matrimonial images from the Bible to the quest for loving union between God and the individual soul. The mysticism of love and union is a mutual and reciprocal attraction between the human person and God. We have a profound need for God, and we experience a lack of fulfillment until that union is achieved. As St. Augustine wrote, "We are made for you, O God, and our hearts are restless until they rest in you."

The path toward union with God is described by the mystics as a process that continually moves a person to a pure love for God. The way of purgation, the way of illumination, and the way of union are necessary elements of that path. St. John of the Cross and St. Theresa of Ávila distinguish between two levels—spiritual betrothal and spiritual marriage—separated by a period of waiting and preparation for full union with God.

St. Bernard of Clairvaux describes this preparation as a process moving through a series of stages: first, from a cringing fear of God, such as that of slaves who obey the master out of fear of punishment; second, to hopeful obedience to God out of expectation of a reward, such as that of a hired servant; third, to the disciplined obedience of a student to a teacher; fourth, to the respectful obedience of a child who knows he is an heir; and finally to the full loving devotion of a bride to her bridegroom (*Sermons on the Song of Songs*, 7).

St. Bernard describes this movement toward union with God as refinement of the human reason by the Word and the refinement of the human will by the Holy Spirit. The Father then joins human reason and will into a perfect soul and "unites it to himself as his glorious bride," from whom the humility of reason has removed all wrinkles and charity of the will has left no stain (*The Twelve Degrees of Humility and of Pride*, 7). "All her being, all her hope, is love and love alone. The bride overflows with love, and therewith the bridegroom is content. He seeks nothing else from her; she has nothing else to give. It is this which makes him the bridegroom and her the bride" (*Sermons on the Song of Songs*, 83).

While this application of mystical and matrimonial symbolism to individual lives can be profitable for spiritual growth, it often fails to express the full richness of the biblical images. Rather, the married couple, living out their mutual love for one another in all its fullness, expresses for us, most clearly and completely, the love between Christ and his church. The love within Christian marriage is a living icon of Christ's spousal love for us. The biblical symbol must maintain its concreteness in the visible world of human love and marriage to maintain its transforming power.

Just as our understanding of baptismal symbolism is diminished if we lose touch with the life-giving effects of flowing water, and eucharistic symbolism is diminished if we lose touch with the bonding effects of family meals, the Bible's matrimonial symbolism loses its richness if it is detached from the context of human commitment and marriage. A biblical or sacramental symbol reveals and makes present what it symbolizes. The symbol or icon of a life-giving marriage evokes God's faithful love for his people and invites our joyful response.

God reveals the qualities of his love for us in and through the experience of spousal love, that exclusive love of spouses for one another with all of its passionate power. This is a love that desires intimacy and union with the other, a love that leads to the highest degree of self-commitment to the other. This love sets aside selfish desires and plants the interests of the other in the center of one's being. Any attempt to claim that this relationship is transitory is rejected as intolerable, and mutual fidelity becomes an imperative. Sacrifice and self-giving for the other are experienced not as an obligation but as a joyful means to express one's love and to deepen that love for the other.

The implications for the church in calling herself the bride of Christ are as numerous as in married life for spouses. From its harsh challenges to its ecstatic joys, matrimonial love expresses in a fresh and exhilarating way the reality of Christ's church. The love of Christ desires this total union, reciprocal and definitive, with his church. The church belongs to Christ, who gave himself completely for her. She has a unique and exclusive relationship with her bridegroom. She was chosen by Christ, and she has accepted that choice. She is clothed in garments that express to the world her relationship with Christ. She has been given gifts to which she must respond, and she longs for the day when her joy will be complete. Christ's bride, the church, lives in hope for that day in which her life and love will be so glorified as to share in perfect mutuality that love with which she is even now loved.

Reflection and discussion

- In what sense is Christian marriage an icon of Christ's spousal love for us?

- How might a study of God's spousal love enhance my understanding of Christian marriage?

Prayer

God of faithful love, who has made Christian marriage as a living icon of your love for us and established the new covenant as the spousal bond of your Son with his church, shower me with your grace as I begin this study of your Scriptures. Let your holy word transform my mind and my heart so that I may respond more fully to the marriage festival of your kingdom. Send your Holy Spirit upon me to guide, encourage, and enlighten me as I contemplate your inspired word.

SUGGESTIONS FOR FACILITATORS, GROUP SESSION 1

1. If the group is meeting for the first time, or if there are newcomers joining the group, it is helpful to provide nametags.

2. Distribute the books to the members of the group.

3. You may want to ask the participants to introduce themselves and tell the group a bit about themselves.

4) Ask one or more of these introductory questions:
   - What drew you to join this group?
   - What is your biggest fear in beginning this Bible study?
   - How is beginning this study like a "threshold" for you?

5. You may want to pray this prayer as a group:

   Come upon us, Holy Spirit, to enlighten and guide us as we begin this study of spousal love. You inspired the biblical authors to express this love as manifested to the people of Israel and most fully in the life of Jesus. Motivate us each day to read the Scriptures and deepen our understanding and love for these sacred texts. Bless us during this session and throughout the coming week with the fire of your love.

6. Read the Introduction aloud, pausing at each question for discussion. Group members may wish to write the insights of the group as each question is discussed. Encourage several members of the group to respond to each question.

7. Don't feel compelled to finish the complete Introduction during the session. It is better to allow sufficient time to talk about the questions raised than to rush to the end. Group members may read any remaining sections on their own after the group meeting.

8. Instruct group members to read the first six lessons on their own during the six days before the next group meeting. They should write out their own answers to the questions as preparation for next week's group discussion.

9. Fill in the date for each group meeting under "Schedule for Group Study."

10. Conclude by praying aloud together the prayer at the end of the Introduction.

**Therefore a man leaves his father and his mother
and clings to his wife, and they become one flesh.** GEN 2:24

Woman Formed from the Side of the Man

GENESIS 2:18–25 ¹⁸*Then the Lord God said, "It is not good that the man should be alone; I will make him a helper as his partner." *¹⁹*So out of the ground the Lord God formed every animal of the field and every bird of the air, and brought them to the man to see what he would call them; and whatever the man called every living creature, that was its name. *²⁰*The man gave names to all cattle, and to the birds of the air, and to every animal of the field; but for the man there was not found a helper as his partner.*

²¹*So the Lord God caused a deep sleep to fall upon the man, and he slept; then he took one of his ribs and closed up its place with flesh.*²²*And the rib that the Lord God had taken from the man he made into a woman and brought her to the man. *²³*Then the man said,*

"This at last is bone of my bones
and flesh of my flesh;
this one shall be called Woman,
for out of Man this one was taken."

²⁴*Therefore a man leaves his father and his mother and clings to his wife, and they become one flesh. *²⁵*And the man and his wife were both naked, and were not ashamed.*

This narrative of humanity's creation in paradise is told in figurative language and images to express the great truths about the human race. The man and woman are God's ideal for humanity, created and desired by God, separate from the compromising reality of sin. So, after creating the various elements of the world, God declared that it is "good," and after completing creation, God saw that it is "very good." But then, in striking contrast, God recognized that it is "not good" that the man should be alone. After identifying this serious exception in God's otherwise ideal environment, God declared that companionship is vital for human thriving.

After God formed the various animals and presented them to the man to examine and name, the man realized that no other creature in the garden fully shared his own nature. So God resolved to make "a helper as his partner" (verses 18, 20). The Hebrew word for "helper" refers to one who assists another. The need for a "helper" implies some type of limitation. It does not suggest that the helper is in any way inferior to the one needing help. In fact, often the helper is superior, as verified by multiple references in Scripture to God as the "helper" of Israel.

The kind of helper and partner needed by the man is one who is of the same essence as the man and who is on the same level. This helping partner will not only contribute distinctively to his life but also provide enriching companionship. God will provide for the man a partner on whom he can pour out the passion that God has put within his heart.

The narrative of woman's creation states that "God caused a deep sleep to come upon the man," and God took one of the ribs of the man and made it into a woman (verses 21–22). Then, like a father of the bride, God leads the woman to the man. The vocabulary stresses that the woman was made of the same substance as the man and according to the same model as the man. Thus, she forms his ideal helper, counterpart, and intimate companion.

The first human words spoken in the Bible are a poem in praise of "Woman" (verse 23). The man exclaims that she is of the same bone and flesh as himself. The lyrical verse speaks of that nearly universal human experience of finding another person with whom one shares such an intense intimacy that it feels as if a lost or unknown part of oneself is being discovered. Here is companionship without superior and inferior, partnership with mutual trust and respect for one another.

This act of creation, the writer explains, is why "a man leaves his father and his mother and clings to his wife" (verse 24). This does not mean that a son no longer has responsibilities to his parents, but it means that he honors his wife, as the central person in his life, with a higher standing. The fact that the man "clings" to his wife does not suggest a suffocating kind of oneness between them or an ensnared unity. Rather, it emphasizes the enduring quality of their bond and their loyalty to each other. Within such a relationship, two partners are secure enough to be their best individual selves. They contribute considerably to each other's life and so grow together as partners.

Likewise, their becoming "one flesh" refers to the kind of physical, social, and spiritual unity the partners achieve together. They become more closely bonded than any of their blood kinship. Marriage joins a man and woman in a covenant of mutual care, tenderness, and devoted love. Because of this faithful and trusting relationship, the two creatures belong together. Any spousal abuse or domination of the other denies the kind of mutuality and harmony that God intends.

This creation account of spousal commitment and unity is encountered in later Hebrew literature as exemplifying God's covenanted love for the Israelites. In the gospels, Jesus refers to these verses when articulating his teaching on marital permanence and fidelity. John's gospel shows that Christ's church is generated from his side after he dies on the cross, just as Woman is created from the man's side while he is in a "deep sleep." The sanctifying water and redeeming blood that flowed from his side creates the sacramental church that becomes, in other New Testament texts, the bride of Christ.

Reflection and discussion
- What does the word "helper" imply about the relationship of spouses to one another?

- What are the truths and sentiments expressed in the lyrical poetry of verse 23?

- What does God's creation of woman from the rib of the man symbolize about their relationship?

- What are the qualities of marriage expressed in this text? How does the reality of human sin flaw this ideal plan of God?

Prayer

Creator God, who made man and woman in your likeness, look upon our fragile, sin-infected humanity with your redeeming grace. Strengthen and preserve your gift of marriage from the effects of our indifferent mind-set and superficial culture. May it become the foundation of a new civilization of love.

Moses took the blood and dashed it on the people, and said, "See the blood of the covenant that the Lord has made with you in accordance with all these words." EXOD 24:8

Israel's Marriage Covenant with God

EXODUS 24:1–11 ¹*Then [God] said to Moses, "Come up to the Lord, you and Aaron, Nadab, and Abihu, and seventy of the elders of Israel, and worship at a distance. ²Moses alone shall come near the Lord; but the others shall not come near, and the people shall not come up with him."*

³*Moses came and told the people all the words of the Lord and all the ordinances; and all the people answered with one voice, and said, "All the words that the Lord has spoken we will do." ⁴And Moses wrote down all the words of the Lord. He rose early in the morning, and built an altar at the foot of the mountain, and set up twelve pillars, corresponding to the twelve tribes of Israel. ⁵He sent young men of the people of Israel, who offered burnt offerings and sacrificed oxen as offerings of well-being to the Lord. ⁶Moses took half of the blood and put it in basins, and half of the blood he dashed against the altar.⁷Then he took the book of the covenant, and read it in the hearing of the people; and they said, "All that the Lord has spoken we will do, and we will be obedient." ⁸Moses took the blood and dashed it on the people, and said, "See the blood of the covenant that the Lord has made with you in accordance with all these words."*

⁹*Then Moses and Aaron, Nadab, and Abihu, and seventy of the elders of Israel went up, ¹⁰and they saw the God of Israel. Under his feet there was something like a pavement of sapphire stone, like the very heaven for clearness. ¹¹God did not lay his hand on the chief men of the people of Israel; also they beheld God, and they ate and drank.*

T his description of the solemn covenant-making ceremony forms the climax of the narrative of Moses at Mount Sinai told in Exod 19—24. As Moses spoke God's words to the people, they respond-ed, "All the words that the Lord has spoken we will do" (verse 3). This ver-bal agreement is then confirmed through several actions. First, Moses wrote down everything, thus formalizing the agreement between God and Israel. Second, Moses built an altar and set up twelve pillars, representing the pres-ence of God and the twelve tribes of Israel (verse 4). Third, Moses sent repre-sentatives to offer holocausts and "offerings of well-being" (*shalom* sacrifices), which the people ate as a sign of communion with God (verse 5).

The blood of the sacrifice both symbolized and contained life. Splashing the blood on the altar, as the fourth covenant-forming action, proclaimed that God was the source of his people's life (verse 6). Fifth, Moses read aloud from the book of the covenant that he had written. After the people listened, they affirmed again their commitment to be obedient to the stipulations of the covenant (verse 7). Finally, Moses took the blood of the covenant and dashed it upon the people saying, "See the blood of the covenant that the Lord has made with you in accordance with all these words" (verse 8). The dashing of blood, both on the altar and on the people, establishes a blood bond, a community of life, between the Lord and Israel. The "blood of the covenant," the sharing of the blood with God, is the seal and pledge of this relationship.

Having established the covenant between God and Israel, Moses and the elders went up the mountain. Their vision of God there is awe-inspiring and full of mystery. God's sovereignty is not compromised by this intimacy. On the mountain they eat and drink, joining in a covenant meal. The divine ef-fulgence indicates a real and personal presence of God with Moses and the leaders of the people as they celebrate the communion meal. This sacrificial, heavenly banquet implies a real sharing of life between the Lord and Israel.

From the perspective of the biblical prophets, what happened on Mount Sinai was nothing less that the marriage of God and Israel. In the Bible a cove-nant is a permanent bond joining people into a family. Through divine words and sacred ritual God entered into a consecrated union, a sacred covenant, with his people. Through the sacrifices and the blood of the covenant, the redeeming God and the twelve tribes of Israel joined themselves in a "flesh and blood" relationship. According to the prophets, this is truly a wedding, in which the Lord of creation is the bridegroom and Israel is his devoted bride. God spoke of this intimate bond through the words of the prophet Ezekiel: "I pledged myself to you and entered into a covenant with you, says the Lord God, and you became mine" (Ezek 16:8).

REFLECTION AND DISCUSSION

- What is the significance of the blood in forming a covenant? In what way does the splashing of blood establish a permanent relationship between God and Israel?

- What elements of the covenant between God and Israel might cause the prophets to describe it as a sacred marriage?

- What elements of this covenant ritual at Sinai have parallels in the ritual of Christian sacramental marriage today?

Prayer

Faithful God, you cared for your people in their bondage and cherished them as you delivered them into the wilderness. You pledged your love to them at the mountain and established your covenant with Israel. Thank you for the intimate and faithful love you show to me.

You shall worship no other god, because the Lord, whose name
is Jealous, is a jealous God. You shall not make a covenant
with the inhabitants of the land. EXOD 34:14–15

Israel's Jealous Spouse

EXODUS 34:5–16 *⁵The Lord descended in the cloud and stood with [Moses] there,
and proclaimed the name, "The Lord." ⁶The Lord passed before him, and proclaimed,*
"The Lord, the Lord,
a God merciful and gracious,
slow to anger,
and abounding in steadfast love and faithfulness,
⁷keeping steadfast love for the thousandth generation,
forgiving iniquity and transgression and sin,
yet by no means clearing the guilty,
but visiting the iniquity of the parents
upon the children
and the children's children,
to the third and the fourth generation."
⁸And Moses quickly bowed his head toward the earth, and worshiped. ⁹He said,
"If now I have found favor in your sight, O Lord, I pray, let the Lord go with us.
Although this is a stiff-necked people, pardon our iniquity and our sin, and take us
for your inheritance."
¹⁰He said: I hereby make a covenant. Before all your people I will perform mar-
vels, such as have not been performed in all the earth or in any nation; and all the
people among whom you live shall see the work of the Lord; for it is an awesome
thing that I will do with you.

¹¹Observe what I command you today. See, I will drive out before you the Amorites, the Canaanites, the Hittites, the Perizzites, the Hivites, and the Jebusites. ¹²Take care not to make a covenant with the inhabitants of the land to which you are going, or it will become a snare among you. ¹³You shall tear down their altars, break their pillars, and cut down their sacred poles ¹⁴(for you shall worship no other god, because the Lord, whose name is Jealous, is a jealous God). ¹⁵You shall not make a covenant with the inhabitants of the land, for when they prostitute themselves to their gods and sacrifice to their gods, someone among them will invite you, and you will eat of the sacrifice. ¹⁶And you will take wives from among their daughters for your sons, and their daughters who prostitute themselves to their gods will make your sons also prostitute themselves to their gods.

Shortly after entering into the covenant with God, the Israelites demonstrated a terrible act of infidelity to the Lord by erecting and worshiping an idol in the form of a golden calf. When the sacred bond between God and his people seemed to be lost, Moses pleaded for the Israelites, and his persuasive arguments led to the amazing reversal of God's intentions. This ability to be persuaded indicates that the divine nature is not static and rigid but is, rather, totally free, personal, and responsive to the changing needs of a vital relationship. Despite the people's sinful infidelity, God does not let them fall into ruin but gives than another opportunity to be covenant partners.

God descended in a cloud to meet Moses on the mountain. There God gave him a new revelation of the divine name and the divine nature. God declares himself to be "merciful and gracious," "slow to anger," "abounding in steadfast love and faithfulness," and having steadfast love that extends hundreds of times farther than his just punishments (verses 6–7). The word translated "steadfast love" implies both tenacious fidelity to a relationship and unrelenting love. It describes God's constant and tender love for Israel, and it expresses God's absolute resolve to continue in loving commitment to those who share the relationship of covenant. Describing God as abounding in "faithfulness" means that he is completely reliable and worthy of Israel's trust.

God's nature had already been demonstrated in the saving events of Israel's liberation from slavery, the deliverance at the sea, nourishment in the wilderness, and covenant on the mountain. Here, God gives Moses assurance of his own personal presence in the continuing journey from the mountain and into the land of promise (verses 9–10). This beautiful declaration of God's nature—proclaiming that God is gracious, merciful, faithful, forgiving, and just—is repeated throughout the Old Testament, especially in the prophets and psalms. This proclamation of God's essence is a summary of God's self-definition, and it became the primary way that God was announced and addressed in Israel's public liturgy.

The covenant God established with Israel had been based on God's wondrous deliverance of Israel from slavery into freedom. The renewed covenant is grounded in an experience just as marvelous. God has delivered Israel from the self-imposed bondage of deadly sin and, through divine forgiveness, brought her back to the experience of freedom that God's presence provides. In the covenant, God's forgiveness, faithfulness, and promises will secure Israel's future. God promises to work awesome "marvels" among the people, but Israel, on her part, must maintain exclusive loyalty in her worship of the Lord. When the people enter the land and become an agricultural people, dependent on abundant fields and fruitful groves, they will be lured by the fertility gods and rituals of other peoples. They must remain faithful to their covenant with the Lord and not be seduced by pagan practices.

The covenant with God creates a sacred boundary. Israel must not enter into any covenant relationships with the other inhabitants of the land and must destroy all the cultic objects associated with their worship (verses 12–13). God's exclusive commitment to his people demands an exclusive commitment in return. The reason for this relationship is the very nature of God: "The Lord, whose name is Jealous, is a jealous God" (verse 14). God's jealousy for Israel requires that she offer her devotion to no other lover.

God's jealousy is an aspect of his spousal love. Of course, in the sinful human condition, jealousy can be selfish and irrational. But as applied to God, jealousy describes the purity of divine love. God's love is not indifferent; rather, it expects and requires a fervent and faithful love in return.

As in a faithless spousal relationship, the dangers of Israel's infidelity to the covenant unfold in phases: first by creating a covenant of mutual advantage with the pagan peoples, then by accepting an invitation to share in their worship, then by eating a sacrifice made to their gods, and finally, by intermarriage with them (verses 15–16). What begins as a simple invitation eventually becomes total betrayal of the covenant and infidelity to God.

Stunningly, the worship of the fertility gods is described in these verses as prostitution, in contrast to the exclusive bond of Israel's spousal covenant with God. Indeed, the fertility rites of Israel's neighbors in the land encouraged sexual decadence. But, more important for Israel, such worship is radically distant from the worship of Israel's God. This idolatry is a repulsive violation of the covenant and betrays Israel's spousal bond with God. Israel has a prior commitment and her divine husband is jealous for the love of his people.

Reflection and discussion

- After the divine self-revelation of verses 6–7, Moses could only bow his head to the ground in worship. What seems astonishing about this description of God?

- God warned Israel that infidelity to the covenant unfolds in phases. In what ways can the bond of marriage gradually disintegrate without vigilance?

Prayer

Lord our God, who is gracious, merciful, faithful, forgiving, and just, I bow in your presence. Teach me to experience your tender and faithful love as you reveal yourself more fully to me. Help me to guard my relationship with you so that I may never betray the bond of love you have offered to me.

The Lord your God will maintain with you the covenant loyalty that he swore to your ancestors; he will love you, bless you, and multiply you; he will bless the fruit of your womb. DEUT 7:12–13

The Blessings of Faithfulness

DEUTERONOMY 7:7–16 ⁷*It was not because you were more numerous than any other people that the Lord set his heart on you and chose you—for you were the fewest of all peoples. ⁸It was because the Lord loved you and kept the oath that he swore to your ancestors, that the Lord has brought you out with a mighty hand, and redeemed you from the house of slavery, from the hand of Pharaoh king of Egypt. ⁹Know therefore that the Lord your God is God, the faithful God who maintains covenant loyalty with those who love him and keep his commandments, to a thousand generations, ¹⁰and who repays in their own person those who reject him. He does not delay but repays in their own person those who reject him. ¹¹Therefore, observe diligently the commandment—the statutes, and the ordinances—that I am commanding you today.*

¹²If you heed these ordinances, by diligently observing them, the Lord your God will maintain with you the covenant loyalty that he swore to your ancestors; ¹³he will love you, bless you, and multiply you; he will bless the fruit of your womb and the fruit of your ground, your grain and your wine and your oil, the increase of your cattle and the issue of your flock, in the land that he swore to your ancestors to give you. ¹⁴You shall be the most blessed of peoples, with neither sterility nor barrenness among you or your livestock. ¹⁵The Lord will turn away from you every illness; all the dread diseases of Egypt that you experienced, he will not inflict on you, but he will lay them on all who hate you. ¹⁶You shall devour all the peoples that the Lord your God is giving over to you, showing them no pity; you shall not serve their gods, for that would be a snare to you.

In the book of Deuteronomy, Moses addresses the Israelites before they cross over into the land God is giving to them. He looks back to the past, recounting their years in the wilderness and the covenant God made with them, and he looks forward to the future, emphasizing the challenges God's people will face in the land and their responsibility to maintain the covenant. In this section, Moses speaks to Israel about why God chose them out of all the peoples on earth to be his own people and about their resultant obligations before God.

Moses says to Israel, "The Lord set his heart on you" (verse 7). In other places in the Old Testament this verb is used for the strong physical desire of a man for a beautiful woman. The phrases indicates, then, that God has the kind of strong desire for Israel that is expressed by a word normally functioning in the human sphere of erotic longing. The same verb is used later in Deuteronomy to state the divine desire even more strongly: although the whole universe belongs to God, "the Lord set his heart in love on your ancestors alone and chose you" (10:14–15).

Yet, quite bluntly, Moses explains that Israel had no special characteristic or attractive quality that elicited such a divine longing. Contrary to what one might expect from the use of this verb, there is in fact nothing in Israel's worth or appearance that should evoke such strong desire from God. The Israelites certainly were not great or numerous, like the Egyptians and the Assyrians. In fact, they were the least and the fewest of all the peoples.

Why, then, did God choose Israel? Moses offers two reasons. First, simply and wonderfully, "It was because the Lord loved you" (verse 8). God's election of Israel is rooted in the inexplicable, self-motivated love of God. Second, the Lord "kept the oath that he swore to your ancestors." God had made promises under oath to the family of Abraham to provide their descendants with land and posterity, and God is faithful to those promises. So God's choice of Israel was based on nothing in themselves that had evoked God's favor, but solely in the love and fidelity of God.

God's choice of Israel out of all the peoples of the earth holds significant implications for Israel's response. Her faith must be a reflection of God's ways with her. The one who loves Israel expects his people to love wholeheartedly in return. The one who faithfully keeps the covenant expects his people to respond with devotion to the stipulations of the covenant (verse 9).

Those who love God by being faithful to the covenant will continue to experience God's steadfast love and covenant fidelity. But those who hate God by their failure to keep the covenant commandments will experience the consequences of that rejection (verse 10). God is reliable and trustworthy to the relationship he has formed with Israel and to his purposes with her. But the hatred of God and disobedience to the covenant of any within Israel thwart God's intentions for Israel and her saving history in the world.

There is no room for an apathetic middle ground: God's people either love him or reject him. When Israel responds positively to God, the opportunities for the fullness of life are abundant beyond all expectation (verses 12–16). There is a powerful link between God's covenant and God's blessings. God's relationship with Israel is enduring and continually expansive. God's covenant loyalty extends to a thousand generations.

Reflection and discussion

• What do the words "The Lord set his heart on you" mean?

• Have I ever experienced this kind of love from God? How could I open my heart to this experience?

- Moses insists that God's love for his people is unconditional, not based on their own merit or worthiness. What is the significance in this for my own relationship with God?

- What are some of the implications of God's loving choice of Israel for her life with God?

- What hope do these words of Moses offer to me?

Prayer

God of faithful love, who chose Israel out of all the peoples of the earth to be your own, you love those who have no attractive qualities to entice you to themselves. May the depth of your unrelenting love and steadfast fidelity give me confidence and hope in my life with you.

Then she shall say, "I will go and return to my first husband, for it was better with me then than now." HOS 2:7

Hosea's Distressed Marriage

HOSEA 1:1—2:7 ¹*The word of the Lord that came to Hosea son of Beeri, in the days of Kings Uzziah, Jotham, Ahaz, and Hezekiah of Judah, and in the days of King Jeroboam son of Joash of Israel.*

²*When the Lord first spoke through Hosea, the Lord said to Hosea, "Go, take for yourself a wife of whoredom and have children of whoredom, for the land commits great whoredom by forsaking the Lord." ³So he went and took Gomer daughter of Diblaim, and she conceived and bore him a son.*

⁴*And the Lord said to him, "Name him Jezreel; for in a little while I will punish the house of Jehu for the blood of Jezreel, and I will put an end to the kingdom of the house of Israel. ⁵On that day I will break the bow of Israel in the valley of Jezreel."*

⁶*She conceived again and bore a daughter. Then the Lord said to him, "Name her Lo-ruhamah, for I will no longer have pity on the house of Israel or forgive them. ⁷But I will have pity on the house of Judah, and I will save them by the Lord their God; I will not save them by bow, or by sword, or by war, or by horses, or by horsemen."*

⁸*When she had weaned Lo-ruhamah, she conceived and bore a son. ⁹Then the Lord said, "Name him Lo-ammi, for you are not my people and I am not your God."*

¹⁰*Yet the number of the people of Israel shall be like the sand of the sea, which can be neither measured nor numbered; and in the place where it was said to them, "You are not my people," it shall be said to them, "Children of the living*

God." ¹¹The people of Judah and the people of Israel shall be gathered together, and they shall appoint for themselves one head; and they shall take possession of the land, for great shall be the day of Jezreel.

2 ¹Say to your brother, Ammi, and to your sister, Ruhamah.
²Plead with your mother, plead—
  for she is not my wife,
    and I am not her husband—
that she put away her whoring from her face,
    and her adultery from between her breasts,
³or I will strip her naked
    and expose her as in the day she was born,
and make her like a wilderness,
    and turn her into a parched land,
    and kill her with thirst.
⁴Upon her children also I will have no pity,
    because they are children of whoredom.
⁵For their mother has played the whore;
    she who conceived them has acted shamefully.
For she said, "I will go after my lovers;
    they give me my bread and my water,
    my wool and my flax, my oil and my drink."
⁶Therefore I will hedge up her way with thorns;
    and I will build a wall against her,
    so that she cannot find her paths.
⁷She shall pursue her lovers,
    but not overtake them;
and she shall seek them,
    but shall not find them.
Then she shall say, "I will go
    and return to my first husband,
    for it was better with me then than now."

Hosea was the first prophet to express God's relationship with Israel using the language and images of a spousal relationship. His prophetic ministry took place in the northern kingdom of Israel in the eighth century BC, during the reign of the five kings mentioned in the opening verse. Although the spirit of rebellion within God's chosen people was present from their beginnings in the wilderness, their disloyalty grows once they begin to live in the promised land and reaches a climactic moment in the period described in Hosea's prophecy.

While Hosea was still a young man, God gave this command: "Go, take for yourself a wife of whoredom and have children of whoredom, for the land commits great whoredom by forsaking the Lord" (1:2). The repetition of this term for sexual promiscuity spotlights the appalling image used to describe the behavior of God's people. When taking Gomer as his wife, the prophet knew of her reputation as a prostitute. Most probably she had participated in the pagan sexual rituals, which were believed to coerce the god Baal into granting fertility to the land. By marrying Gomer, he became a prophetic sign that God too is married to an unfaithful harlot. Gomer herself became a prophetic sign of Israel's participation in the religion of Baal.

The three children born to Gomer express the results of such a promiscuous marriage. The naming of these children symbolically announces the judgment of God upon Israel and demonstrates a shocking progression. God commands that the first child be named "Jezreel." This fertile valley where the worship of Baal flourished will become the place where Israel will be defeated by the invading armies of Assyria (1:4–5). God orders that the second child be named "Lo-ruhamah," meaning "Not-pitied." The tender pity that God had for his people has changed to indifference because of their constant betrayal (1:6). Finally, God commands his prophet to name the third child "Lo-ammi," meaning "Not my people." The covenant that made Israel the people of God is no longer effective (1:9). God's patient forgiveness has come to an end, and Israel will be overrun by her enemies.

Hosea spoke his prophecy and also enacted it. For him there was no separation between his prophetic calling and his family life. Because of Hosea's own heart-wrenching experiences with his wife and children, he is able to describe the agony in the heart of God like no other prophet. His own emotional pain has become a parable of the divine anguish over unfaithful and ungrateful Israel.

Immediately after this declaration of doom, the prophet begins an announcement of hope. Beyond the immediate tragedy will come a reversal of Israel's fate and a bright future (1:10–11). Israel's population will number as many as the sands of the sea, the covenant will be restored, and the southern kingdom (Judah) and the northern kingdom (Israel) will be reunited under one "head." All of this will take place on the day of "Jezreel," which literally means, "God sows." Abundance and fertility in the land will return to God's people. God indeed is the source of Israel's life, not the pagan fertility religion. The significance of the names of the three children has been reversed: "God sows," "My people," and "Pitied" express God's future relationship with Israel (2:1).

Moving back to the present reality, the husband pleads his case. Yet even as he disowns his spouse, he yearns for her. Because there is little likelihood that she will listen to him, he pleads with her indirectly through her children (2:2). Her scandalous violations of their marriage have provoked the rage and anguish of her husband. God's shocking accusation is made clearly evident to Israel through Hosea's own heartache as a husband married to an adulterous woman.

Israel has acted shamefully, pursuing lovers that are not her husband (2:5). She is convinced that they can give her a life of abundance. But the one who loves her still calls to her and desires her return. He will discredit the fertility gods by withholding her prosperity. Her deprivation will be so severe that she will realize that she would be better off with her original husband (2:6–7). Perhaps the memories of Israel's earlier history—the nourishment, pleasure, and closeness with her God—will reawaken a hope that what has been lost might be restored.

Reflection and discussion

- What are some of the ways in which Hosea expresses the "jealousy" of God?

- In what ways does Hosea's marriage boldly demonstrate the significance of Israel's infidelity to the covenant?

- How does Hosea help me to see the tragedy of my own sin as an expression of disloyalty to God?

- What are some of the reasons why married couples can become estranged? What can couples do to maintain a strong bond of commitment?

Prayer

Faithful and loving Spouse, who never gives up on your people, continue to pursue me despite my neglect of you. Show me the ways that I have failed to fulfill the covenant and have been unfaithful to the relationship you have formed with me. Give me the grace of repentance.

I will take you for my wife forever; I will take you for my wife in righteousness and in justice, in steadfast love, and in mercy. HOS 2:19

God Will Renew the Divine Marriage with Israel

HOSEA 2:14–23 ¹⁴*Therefore, I will now allure her,*
and bring her into the wilderness,
and speak tenderly to her.
¹⁵*From there I will give her her vineyards,*
and make the Valley of Achor a door of hope.
There she shall respond as in the days of her youth,
as at the time when she came out of the land of Egypt.
¹⁶*On that day, says the Lord, you will call me, "My husband," and no longer will you call me, "My Baal." *¹⁷*For I will remove the names of the Baals from her mouth, and they shall be mentioned by name no more. *¹⁸*I will make for you a covenant on that day with the wild animals, the birds of the air, and the creeping things of the ground; and I will abolish the bow, the sword, and war from the land; and I will make you lie down in safety. *¹⁹*And I will take you for my wife forever; I will take you for my wife in righteousness and in justice, in steadfast love, and in mercy. *²⁰*I will take you for my wife in faithfulness; and you shall know the Lord.*
²¹*On that day I will answer, says the Lord,*
I will answer the heavens
and they shall answer the earth;
²²*and the earth shall answer the grain, the wine, and the oil,*
and they shall answer Jezreel;

²³and I will sow him for myself in the land.
And I will have pity on Lo-ruhamah,
and I will say to Lo-ammi, "You are my people";
and he shall say, "You are my God."

I n any committed relationship, the feelings of falling in love are impossible to maintain. The challenge of marriage is channeling the passion of youth into a mature and lasting love. Like the marriage of Hosea and Gomer, God and Israel had become estranged. Yet, just as the heart of Hosea longed for his spouse, God still cherished his beloved. Although the dedicated love of God made known in the exodus and at Mount Sinai seemed remote, God expressed his determination to rekindle the romance they enjoyed in their early years together.

Behind all these words of the prophet there is a divine love that will not let go of faithless Israel. One day, God and his people will reunite and their relationship will begin again. God will bring Israel into the wilderness as he did when he first freed her from the bonds of Egypt. There, where no Baal can come between them, God will "speak tenderly to her" and woo the heart of his bride back to himself (verse 14). God will give her vineyards and fertile valleys. God's people will respond to God as in those days when their love was young and grew into a committed covenant (verse 15). With genuine repentance and single-heartedness, Israel will affirm God for who he truly is, calling him "My husband" (verse 16).

God promises security for Israel, consisting of a new harmony with the creatures of the natural world and the abolition of weapons of war from the land (verse 18). Then, having assured Israel of her safety and established a bond of trust, God will enter into a formal betrothal with his beloved people, a faithful and lasting marital covenant (verse 19). The Lord pledges to bestow upon his wife the gifts of righteousness, justice, steadfast love, mercy, and faithfulness. Then, Israel will truly "know the Lord," a key expression in the writing of Hosea to describe the intimate relationship and mutual devotion between God and his people (verse 20).

The establishment of this new and everlasting marital covenant will come about in the messianic age of God's kingdom. In those days, the new Israel will lack for nothing. The Lord will call the heavens to bring forth rain, and the earth will give forth grain, grapes, and olives, crying out with joy, "Jezreel," that is, "God sows" (verse 22). God will again have pity on his people and restore the covenant, saying to them, "You are my people," and they will respond with trust and surrender, "You are my God." The age of the new covenant will gather up all the promises of God to his people of old and bring them to completion.

Reflection and discussion

- According to Hosea, what will be new about the covenant that God will make with his people in the future?

- What might Hosea have to teach young couples about the importance of maintaining a strong and resilient marriage?

- Marriage counselors will often ask couples in a troubled relationship, "What made you first fall in love with your spouse?" Why might this be a helpful question for estranged couples to consider?

Prayer

God of unrelenting fidelity, your affection for me and your desire for me to return your love are greater than I can imagine. Deepen your gifts of righteousness, justice, steadfast love, mercy, and faithfulness within me so that I may respond with trusting confidence in you.

SUGGESTIONS FOR FACILITATORS, GROUP SESSION 2

1. If there are newcomers who were not present for the first group session, introduce them now.

2. You may want to pray this prayer as a group:
   Faithful God, you showed your steadfast love to Israel in their bondage and deliverance, and you established your covenant as a promise of unending devotion. Show us the ways we have betrayed your faithfulness, and give us the grace of repentance. Help us continually respond to your spousal covenant with gratitude and trusting confidence in you. As we study these ancient Scriptures, open our hearts to your word as you reveal yourself more fully and teach us how to love.

3. Ask one or more of the following questions:
   - What was your biggest challenge in Bible study over this past week?
   - What did you learn about God's love from your study this week?
   - What did you learn about yourself this week?

4. Discuss lessons 1 through 6 together. Assuming that group members have read the Scripture and commentary during the week, there is no need to read it aloud. As you review each lesson, you might want to briefly summarize the Scripture passages of each lesson and ask the group what stands out most clearly from the commentary.

5. Choose one or more of the questions for reflection and discussion from each lesson to talk over as a group. You may want to ask group members which question was most challenging or helpful to them as you review each lesson.

6. Keep the discussion moving, but don't rush the discussion in order to complete more questions. Allow time for the questions that provoke the most discussion.

7. Instruct group members to complete lessons 7 through 12 on their own during the six days before the next group meeting. They should write out their own answers to the questions as preparation for next week's group discussion.

8. Conclude by praying aloud together the prayer at the end of lesson 6, or any other prayer you choose.

There shall once more be heard the voice of mirth and the voice of gladness, the voice of the bridegroom and the voice of the bride, the voices of those who sing, as they bring thank offerings to the house of the Lord. JER 33:10–11

Israel's Divine Husband Promises a New Covenant

JEREMIAH 31:31–34 *³¹The days are surely coming, says the Lord, when I will make a new covenant with the house of Israel and the house of Judah. ³²It will not be like the covenant that I made with their ancestors when I took them by the hand to bring them out of the land of Egypt—a covenant that they broke, though I was their husband, says the Lord. ³³But this is the covenant that I will make with the house of Israel after those days, says the Lord: I will put my law within them, and I will write it on their hearts; and I will be their God, and they shall be my people. ³⁴No longer shall they teach one another, or say to each other, "Know the Lord," for they shall all know me, from the least of them to the greatest, says the Lord; for I will forgive their iniquity, and remember their sin no more.*

JEREMIAH 33:10–18 *¹⁰Thus says the Lord: In this place of which you say, "It is a waste without human beings or animals," in the towns of Judah and the streets of Jerusalem that are desolate, without inhabitants, human or animal, there shall once more be heard ¹¹the voice of mirth and the voice of gladness, the voice of the bridegroom and the voice of the bride, the voices of those who sing, as they bring thank offerings to the house of the Lord:*

"Give thanks to the Lord of hosts,

for the Lord is good,
for his steadfast love endures forever!"
For I will restore the fortunes of the land as at first, says the Lord.

¹²Thus says the Lord of hosts: In this place that is waste, without human beings or animals, and in all its towns there shall again be pasture for shepherds resting their flocks. ¹³In the towns of the hill country, of the Shephelah, and of the Negeb, in the land of Benjamin, the places around Jerusalem, and in the towns of Judah, flocks shall again pass under the hands of the one who counts them, says the Lord.

¹⁴The days are surely coming, says the Lord, when I will fulfill the promise I made to the house of Israel and the house of Judah. ¹⁵In those days and at that time I will cause a righteous Branch to spring up for David; and he shall execute justice and righteousness in the land. ¹⁶In those days Judah will be saved and Jerusalem will live in safety. And this is the name by which it will be called: "The Lord is our righteousness."

¹⁷For thus says the Lord: David shall never lack a man to sit on the throne of the house of Israel, ¹⁸and the levitical priests shall never lack a man in my presence to offer burnt offerings, to make grain offerings, and to make sacrifices for all time.

The prophet Jeremiah spoke in the days after the Babylonians had defeated Judah, the southern kingdom, and destroyed the city of Jerusalem. He described the promised land as "a waste," a desolate land, without inhabitants in its towns or flocks in its fields (33:10). The Babylonians had destroyed the temple and deported the king, bringing an end to the priesthood and monarchy, the two most tangible expressions of God's presence with his people. Without these two visible institutions, could Israel continue to regard herself as the people of God?

But into this wasteland, Jeremiah's prophecy speaks words of hope for the future: "The days are surely coming, says the Lord" (31:31; 33:14). In those days the sounds of laughter and joy, "the voice of the bridegroom and the voice of the bride," will return to the land. Because God's love is always faithful, he will restore blessings to the land and its people (33:11). Again, shepherds will pasture and count their flocks and rest with them in the land of Judah (33:12).

In addition to a joyful and plenteous future, God will fulfill the assurances he made to "the house of Israel and the house of Judah"—the twelve tribes of reunited Israel (31:31; 33:14). God's promises that a successor of King David will always sit on his throne will be accomplished through the "righteous Branch," the messiah from David's line (33:15, 17). God's promises of a continuing priesthood for offering sacrifice will also be accomplished in the future days (33:18).

These messianic prophecies are accompanied by Jeremiah's oracle of the "new covenant" with God's reunited people (31:31). This covenant will be radically different from that made by God with Israel on Mount Sinai. Even though God had become Israel's "husband," Israel had broken this covenant (31:32), as evidenced by the devastation of the land, the temple, and the priesthood. Whether this broken covenant results in permanent divorce or a restoration of the marriage depends on the heart of God and the hearts of his people.

Will the wronged partners walk away forever? Will they just pretend that nothing ever happened? Or could the partners possibly forgive what has been done and begin the covenant on new grounds? Through the power of God's merciful love, the God of Israel decides, "I will forgive their iniquity, and remember their sin no more" (31:34). The first covenant is not annulled; rather, it is renewed and expanded. This new covenant in the days to come will be written, not on stone, but on the hearts of God's people. Thus, it will be an unbreakable relationship. Israel will know God and desire God's ways from their inmost selves because God will wondrously change the hearts of his people with his creative grace. At last, the grounds are established for an indissoluble marriage with all its delights.

The New Testament teaches that this new king and new priesthood has entered the world with Jesus. He inaugurated the new and everlasting covenant on the eve of his death, as he gave the cup to his disciples with these words: "This cup that is poured out for you is the new covenant in my blood" (Luke 22:20). The new king and new priest offered the perfect sacrifice on the cross and offered his blood for the forgiveness of sins. With this new covenant, the prophecies are fulfilled, and all people, from the least to the greatest, will come to know the Lord with a rightly directed heart.

Reflection and discussion

- What are some of the ways that God's promises made through Jeremiah have been fulfilled among us?

- What is the same and what is different from the old covenant to the new covenant?

- What does the forgiveness of God do to the hearts of his people? How can the power of God's forgiveness heal broken and struggling marriages?

Prayer

Divine Lover, through your prophets you taught your people to await a new covenant, an intimate and permanent bond with you. Transform my heart so that I may experience a deeper desire to know you and to respond to your will.

I will remember my covenant with you in the days of your youth,
and I will establish with you an everlasting covenant.
Then you will remember your ways. EZEK 16:60-61

God Will Forgive His Unfaithful Spouse

EZEKIEL 16:1–22, 59–63 *¹The word of the Lord came to me: ²Mortal, make known to Jerusalem her abominations, ³and say, Thus says the Lord God to Jerusalem: Your origin and your birth were in the land of the Canaanites; your father was an Amorite, and your mother a Hittite. ⁴As for your birth, on the day you were born your navel cord was not cut, nor were you washed with water to cleanse you, nor rubbed with salt, nor wrapped in cloths. ⁵No eye pitied you, to do any of these things for you out of compassion for you; but you were thrown out in the open field, for you were abhorred on the day you were born.*

⁶I passed by you, and saw you flailing about in your blood. As you lay in your blood, I said to you, "Live! ⁷and grow up like a plant of the field." You grew up and became tall and arrived at full womanhood; your breasts were formed, and your hair had grown; yet you were naked and bare.

⁸I passed by you again and looked on you; you were at the age for love. I spread the edge of my cloak over you, and covered your nakedness: I pledged myself to you and entered into a covenant with you, says the Lord God, and you became mine. ⁹Then I bathed you with water and washed off the blood from you, and anointed you with oil. ¹⁰I clothed you with embroidered cloth and with sandals of fine leather; I bound you in fine linen and covered you with rich fabric. ¹¹I adorned you with ornaments: I put bracelets on your arms, a chain on your neck, ¹²a ring

on your nose, earrings in your ears, and a beautiful crown upon your head. ¹³You
were adorned with gold and silver, while your clothing was of fine linen, rich fabric,
and embroidered cloth. You had choice flour and honey and oil for food. You grew
exceedingly beautiful, fit to be a queen. ¹⁴Your fame spread among the nations on
account of your beauty, for it was perfect because of my splendor that I had bestowed on you, says the Lord God.

¹⁵But you trusted in your beauty, and played the whore because of your fame, and
lavished your whorings on any passer-by. ¹⁶You took some of your garments, and
made for yourself colorful shrines, and on them played the whore; nothing like this
has ever been or ever shall be.¹⁷You also took your beautiful jewels of my gold and
my silver that I had given you, and made for yourself male images, and with them
played the whore; ¹⁸and you took your embroidered garments to cover them, and set
my oil and my incense before them. ¹⁹Also my bread that I gave you—I fed you with
choice flour and oil and honey—you set it before them as a pleasing odor; and so it
was, says the Lord God. ²⁰You took your sons and your daughters, whom you had
borne to me, and these you sacrificed to them to be devoured. As if your whorings
were not enough! ²¹You slaughtered my children and delivered them up as an offering
to them. ²²And in all your abominations and your whorings you did not remember
the days of your youth, when you were naked and bare, flailing about in your blood.

⁵⁹Yes, thus says the Lord God: I will deal with you as you have done, you who
have despised the oath, breaking the covenant; ⁶⁰yet I will remember my covenant
with you in the days of your youth, and I will establish with you an everlasting
covenant. ⁶¹Then you will remember your ways, and be ashamed when I take your
sisters, both your elder and your younger, and give them to you as daughters, but
not on account of my covenant with you. ⁶²I will establish my covenant with you,
and you shall know that I am the Lord, ⁶³in order that you may remember and
be confounded, and never open your mouth again because of your shame, when I
forgive you all that you have done, says the Lord God.

The prophet Ezekiel develops a drama of love between God and
Jerusalem, told with lavish imagery in distinct stages. Jerusalem represents all of God's people, just as Israel did in the writings of Hosea
and Jeremiah. Using the metaphor of the marriage covenant, Ezekiel tells the

story of youthful love, shameful betrayal, and costly redemption. In telling the story of Jerusalem's life, the prophet's criticism of God's people takes them down into the condition of their exile, while his promises lift them up to their final destination.

The extended imagery begins with a description of Jerusalem's parentage and birth. Jerusalem, the prophet insists, was not originally an Israelite city but had its origins in the pagan cultures of Canaan (verse 3). At her birth, she remained unwashed, her umbilical cord uncut, not rubbed with salt to promote circulation or wrapped in swaddling clothes—all the customary procedures for welcoming newborns into the world (verse 4). When God first "passed by" the newly born Jerusalem, she was unwanted and abandoned, flailing about in her own blood (verses 5–6). But God rescued the forsaken foundling, calling to her, "Live!" And life flowed into the child, enabling her to grow up and mature.

The next time God "passed by," Jerusalem had become a young woman and was "at the age for love" (verse 8). The image of God changes from rescuer to suitor and spouse. Spreading the edge of his cloak over her signified a commitment to marry her. God then entered into a covenant with her, claiming her as his own. After cleansing Jerusalem of her impurity, God clothed her lavishly and adorned her in jewelry (verses 9–14). The preparation for marriage is described in terms of a royal wedding. God loved Jerusalem with a generosity not shown to any other people. She became "fit to be a queen," renowned among the nations for her extraordinary beauty.

But Jerusalem's pride and idolatry led to her ruin. Rather than trusting in the Lord, her husband, Jerusalem became a prostitute, worshiping the idols of other nations. God accuses her of using her colorful garments and beautiful jewelry to create idols for worship (verses 15–19). He even charges her with offering their children for child sacrifice, the most horrendous of the Canaanite religious practices (verses 20–21). Jerusalem had forgotten her desperate beginnings and rejected the God who is the source of her life and of all that she has (verse 22).

Ezekiel's drama concludes with both the inevitability of God's judgment and the assurance of God's fidelity. Although the consequences of Jerusalem's betrayal of the covenant will come upon her, God will remember the covenant he made with his people and will establish an "everlasting covenant" (verses

59–60). Rather than looking back to better days of long ago, God focuses his people ahead to the future. After the exile is over and God's people are united again in their own land, God will create a marriage bond that will last forever.

In this new spousal relationship, God will not only restore Jerusalem but praise and honor her as well. God will make the cities that were formerly Jerusalem's sister-cities—like Samaria and Sodom—her daughters (verse 61). But none of this will happen because of any merit on the part of Jerusalem, but only because God will "forgive" all that Jerusalem has done (verse 63). This undeserved forgiveness will jar Jerusalem's memories and cause her to be speechless at her disloyalty and to feel shame for her past betrayals.

Reflection and discussion

- What are some of the feelings God's people might have experienced as Ezekiel spoke these words describing their relationship with God?

- Why would the people of Jerusalem be stunned when told that God will forgive all that they have done? What helps me to realize the astounding and undeserved love of God for me?

Prayer

How great is your love for me, O God. You have loved me from the beginning of my life and lavished me with unearned and undeserved gifts. May I stand in speechless disbelief that I would ever forget or betray your faithful covenant.

In overflowing wrath for a moment I hid my face from you,
but with everlasting love I will have compassion on you,
says the Lord, your Redeemer. ISA 54:8

God's Spousal Love
Is Everlasting

ISAIAH 54:1–10   *¹Sing, O barren one who did not bear;*
  burst into song and shout,
  you who have not been in labor!
For the children of the desolate woman will be more
  than the children of her that is married, says the Lord.
²Enlarge the site of your tent,
  and let the curtains of your habitations be stretched out;
do not hold back; lengthen your cords
  and strengthen your stakes.
³For you will spread out to the right and to the left,
  and your descendants will possess the nations
  and will settle the desolate towns.
    ⁴Do not fear, for you will not be ashamed;
  do not be discouraged, for you will not suffer disgrace;
for you will forget the shame of your youth,
  and the disgrace of your widowhood you will remember no more.
⁵For your Maker is your husband,
  the Lord of hosts is his name;
the Holy One of Israel is your Redeemer,

43

the God of the whole earth he is called.
⁶For the Lord has called you
  like a wife forsaken and grieved in spirit,
like the wife of a man's youth when she is cast off,
  says your God.
⁷For a brief moment I abandoned you,
  but with great compassion I will gather you.
⁸In overflowing wrath for a moment
  I hid my face from you,
but with everlasting love I will have compassion on you,
  says the Lord, your Redeemer.
⁹This is like the days of Noah to me:
  Just as I swore that the waters of Noah
  would never again go over the earth,
so I have sworn that I will not be angry with you
  and will not rebuke you.
¹⁰For the mountains may depart
  and the hills be removed,
but my steadfast love shall not depart from you,
  and my covenant of peace shall not be removed,
  says the Lord, who has compassion on you.

The prophet offers images of devastating disappointments to address the situation of God's people: childlessness, widowhood, abandonment, and divorce. Anyone who has suffered such losses within the context of marriage and family life connects on a deeply personal level with the emotional pain in these passages. The setting of Isaiah's prophecy, the destruction of Jerusalem and the exile of God's people in Babylon, is a time of deep emotional loss for God's people. Jerusalem is cast in the role of a barren woman and a forsaken wife. She laments that she has been humiliated, that God has deserted and forgotten her. She feels that her troubles are due to her abandonment by her husband. She is "like a wife forsaken and grieved," like a wife "when she is cast off" (verse 6).

God responds by calling his barren wife to "sing" (verse 1). Her children will be so numerous that there will hardly be room for them. She must en-large the size of the family tent, adding new sections, lengthening the ropes, and strengthening the stakes to support the larger dwelling (verse 2). The family of the formerly childless wife will spread out in all directions and in-herit the whole land (verse 3).

The Lord proclaims that Jerusalem's humiliation is at an end. She need not fear or be discouraged, for she will forget her shame and disgrace. How can she know this? Because the husband whose absence she laments is Israel's Maker; because "the Holy One of Israel" is also "the God of the whole earth" (verse 5). To Israel's complaint that the Lord has forsaken her, God replies with assurances of steadfast love. Like a good husband, the Lord does not blame the other or deny the real pain that their separation has caused. Rather, God contrasts the "brief moment" in which he "abandoned" Israel with the "great compassion" with which he will take her back (verse 7). He distinguishes the "overflowing wrath" that lasted only "for a moment" from the "everlasting love" with which he will have compassion on his beloved (verse 8). A more beauti-ful expression of enduring love would be difficult to find in any literature.

Jerusalem wants to know how she can be sure that God's wrath has been overcome by everlasting love. God must further reassure her by providing a guarantee that the catastrophe will not just continue to repeat itself. So the Lord recalls the story of Noah and the divine pledge never to destroy the earth again. Like God's pledge to Noah, God pledges that he will not remain angry with Jerusalem nor will he rebuke her (verse 9). The story of Noah becomes the basis for God's incredible promise: "For the mountains may depart and the hills be removed, but my steadfast love shall not depart from you, and my covenant of peace shall not be removed" (verse 10). God's words are filled with passion and conviction. Not only is God a dependable and trustworthy husband; truly God has compassion on his people and guides their history in order to redeem them.

The words of the prophet recall a time of deep suffering for God's people. But in retrospect, even the disaster of Israel's exile became an aspect of God's mercy for his people. Through the exile, God's people would be purified of their idolatry and injustices, thus becoming more able once again to enter into an intimate relationship with the Lord. Likewise, we can understand even the painful adversity of our lives as an aspect of God's faithful love toward us. For God cares for us with deep compassion and with an everlasting love.

Reflection and discussion

- What circumstances made God's people feel like a barren woman and an abandoned wife?

- How have I experienced God drawing me back to himself after a time of separation?

- What aspects of God's relationship to Jerusalem in these verses could be helpfully explored by spouses?

Prayer

Holy One of Israel, you are eternally faithful to your people and your compassion is without limit. Use my painful experiences to draw me to yourself. Help me to trust in your faithful love and to see your hand at work even in my adversity and failures.

For as a young man marries a young woman, so shall your builder marry you, and as the bridegroom rejoices over the bride, so shall your God rejoice over you. ISA 62:5

The Bridegroom Will Rejoice Over His Bride

ISAIAH 61:10—62:5 *¹⁰I will greatly rejoice in the Lord,*
my whole being shall exult in my God;
for he has clothed me with the garments of salvation,
he has covered me with the robe of righteousness,
as a bridegroom decks himself with a garland,
and as a bride adorns herself with her jewels.
¹¹For as the earth brings forth its shoots,
and as a garden causes what is sown in it to spring up,
so the Lord God will cause righteousness and praise
to spring up before all the nations.

62 *¹For Zion's sake I will not keep silent,*
and for Jerusalem's sake I will not rest,
until her vindication shines out like the dawn,
and her salvation like a burning torch.
²The nations shall see your vindication,
and all the kings your glory;
and you shall be called by a new name
that the mouth of the Lord will give.

³You shall be a crown of beauty in the hand of the Lord,
*   and a royal diadem in the hand of your God.*
⁴You shall no more be termed Forsaken,
*   and your land shall no more be termed Desolate;*
but you shall be called My Delight Is in Her,
*   and your land Married;*
for the Lord delights in you,
*   and your land shall be married.*
⁵For as a young man marries a young woman,
*   so shall your builder marry you,*
and as the bridegroom rejoices over the bride,
*   so shall your God rejoice over you.*

The prophet is filled with rejoicing on behalf of God's people. Zion/ Jerusalem has come up out of the ashes of destruction as a result of God's faithful love. While the prophet delights in what the Lord has done, his jubilation is even greater for what more God will still do. The prophecy looks forward to salvation being fully accomplished and bestowed on Jerusalem.

The prophet speaks in the name of the one who has said, "The spirit of the Lord God is upon me, because the Lord has anointed me" (61:1). God will clothe this anointed one (and through him all of God's people) with the garments of salvation and righteousness (61:10). "Salvation" is the work of God directed toward his people; "righteousness" is the result of God's saving work in his people. God's salvation bestowed on Jerusalem bears the fruit of righteousness in those who receive it.

The garments of salvation and righteousness are compared with the clothing of a bridegroom and his bride. The garment of salvation is the garb of the anointed one, the bridegroom; the robe of righteousness is the attire of Jerusalem, the bride. The bride and bridegroom are adorned, and all seems ready for the wedding.

This promise of God to restore his people is as reliable as the tender shoots that grow up in season from a sown garden (61:11). Righteousness and praise among God's people is the fruit of God's cultivating care as he keeps his promises. When this righteousness and praise springs forth, as it most certainly will, it will be seen by all the nations of the earth.

The prophet then takes on a spirit of confident urgency. He will speak and act as intercessor for God's people, insisting that God bring forth the salvation of Zion/Jerusalem (62:1–2). He knows that this gift of God to his people will attract the attention of the world: all kings and nations will witness this gift of God, like the dawn rising from the night or like a burning torch in the darkness. This salvation will give to God's people a royal dignity: they will be valuable and precious to God, like the crown of a king (62:3). Jerusalem will be the sign that the Lord is king.

Spousal images are used to express the new names given to Jerusalem, expressions of her new status and potential (62:4). Both God's people and their land are given names because salvation effects change in both the people and their environment. Jerusalem is no longer called Forsaken and her land called Desolate, as she was thought of by herself and as she was seen by others. She will be called "My Delight Is in Her" and her land will be called "Married."

The climactic promise expresses the jubilation of God's salvation in terms of the commitments of a wedding and the delights of married life (62:5). Like the marriage of a young man and woman, Jerusalem's divine builder will enter the marriage covenant with her. As the bridegroom rejoices over the bride, so God will give the fullness of life to his people in their everlasting covenant.

Reflection and discussion

- How is my relationship with God challenged by God's use of the bride and groom imagery?

- Why are spousal images of courtship, betrothal, betrayal, abandonment, commitment, and marriage such effective ways to express the dynamics of God's relationship with his people?

- In what ways do names and nicknames express the status and potential of people? What might these prophetic names do for God's people?

- In what ways is a spirit of confident urgency important for a marriage? How could the words of Isaiah be encouraging for married couples?

Prayer

Lord God, who rejoices over your people and delights in them, bring forth your salvation so that all peoples and nations can see how you cherish those who trust in you. As a bridegroom rejoices over the bride, may you delight in me as I long for your saving love.

In many-colored robes she is led to the king; behind her the virgins, her companions, follow. With joy and gladness they are led along as they enter the palace of the king. PS 45:14–15

The King's Royal Wedding

PSALM 45 *¹My heart overflows with a goodly theme;*
I address my verses to the king;
my tongue is like the pen of a ready scribe.

²You are the most handsome of men;
grace is poured upon your lips;
therefore God has blessed you forever.
³Gird your sword on your thigh, O mighty one,
in your glory and majesty.

⁴In your majesty ride on victoriously
for the cause of truth and to defend the right;
let your right hand teach you dread deeds.
⁵Your arrows are sharp
in the heart of the king's enemies;
the peoples fall under you.

⁶Your throne, O God, endures forever and ever.
Your royal scepter is a scepter of equity;
⁷you love righteousness and hate wickedness.
Therefore God, your God, has anointed you

with the oil of gladness beyond your companions;
 ⁸your robes are all fragrant with myrrh and aloes and cassia.
From ivory palaces stringed instruments make you glad;
 ⁹daughters of kings are among your ladies of honor;
 at your right hand stands the queen in gold of Ophir.

¹⁰Hear, O daughter, consider and incline your ear;
 forget your people and your father's house,
 ¹¹and the king will desire your beauty.
Since he is your lord, bow to him;
 ¹²the people of Tyre will seek your favor with gifts,
 the richest of the people ¹³with all kinds of wealth.

The princess is decked in her chamber with gold-woven robes;
 ¹⁴in many-colored robes she is led to the king;
 behind her the virgins, her companions, follow.
¹⁵With joy and gladness they are led along
 as they enter the palace of the king.

¹⁶In the place of ancestors you, O king, shall have sons;
 you will make them princes in all the earth.
 ¹⁷I will cause your name to be celebrated in all generations;
 therefore the peoples will praise you forever and ever.

This psalm was composed for a royal marriage, perhaps for a wedding of King Solomon or another king from the line of King David. It was later interpreted as a psalm about God's anointed one who would bring salvation to Israel in future days. In the era of the New Testament, Christians began to pray the psalm as an expression of the actions of Christ, the royal bridegroom, in relationship to his church.

The psalm begins with the introductory words of the speaker, perhaps the best man, who will address words of homage to the king and his bride (verse 1). The speaker then compliments the king on his handsome appearance and his excellence in speaking (verse 2). As commander of Israel's armed forces, the king is majestic in military array, but he must only go into battle for the cause of truth and right for his people (verses 3–5).

The king sits on the throne of God, ruling Israel on God's behalf. As a descendant of David's line, the king holds a reign that will last forever. As a representative of God's rule, he governs with fairness, justice, and righteousness (verses 6–7). Because of the king's commitment to these virtues, God has chosen him and anointed him. He is robed in scented garments, with stringed instruments playing within his palace, and with princesses within his court. The "queen," the mother of the reigning king, stands to his right in royal ceremonies (verses 8–9).

The speaker then turns to address the bride. She is evidently from a different country, as were many brides of Israel's kings. She is urged to forget her own people and family. Like Ruth, she must leave her own culture, loyalties, and religion, so that she may take on those of her husband (verse 10). The king's authority seems to carry over into the marriage, since his bride is urged to bow to him, recognizing him as both husband and monarch (verse 11).

Because of the bride's new title, people of foreign lands bring her gifts and riches (verses 12–14). The speaker offers an eloquent description of how the bride looks as she is led to the chamber of the king, adorned in multicolored robes woven with gold. Her retinue of bridesmaids follows behind her in joyful celebration.

The consummation of the union of the king and his bride brings the hope of offspring through whom his rule will be extended in all the earth (verse 16). The direct address of the speaker to the king returns with a flourish in the final verse (verse 17). He promises that he will cause the king's name to be "celebrated in all generations" and praised forever.

The psalm inevitably was read by later generations as a messianic text. The writer of the book of Hebrews found here the language to express the person and mission of Christ, in whom God's anointed king is perfectly embodied (Heb 1:8–9). The psalm became a popular wedding song because it reflects the dignity of marriage and its potential to reflect the devoted love of Christ for his church.

Reflection and discussion

- What are some of my favorite memories of weddings I have witnessed?

- How does the experience of being truly loved help me "forget" all other relationships? What must I "forget" in order to truly honor my Lord?

- This psalm is often sung in Jewish and Christian weddings. What qualities of the bride and groom seem to be especially praised in this wedding hymn?

Prayer

Bridegroom of the church, inspire me to follow your fidelity and your love of justice. Deepen my desire to praise your name in every generation and throughout all the earth.

Look, O daughters of Zion, at King Solomon, at the crown with which his mother crowned him on the day of his wedding, on the day of the gladness of his heart. SONG 3:11

Song of the King and His Beloved

SONG OF SONGS 2:8–13

⁸*The voice of my beloved!*
  Look, he comes,
leaping upon the mountains,
  bounding over the hills.
⁹*My beloved is like a gazelle*
  or a young stag.
Look, there he stands
  behind our wall,
gazing in at the windows,
  looking through the lattice.
¹⁰*My beloved speaks and says to me:*
"Arise, my love, my fair one,
  and come away;
¹¹*for now the winter is past,*
  the rain is over and gone.
¹²*The flowers appear on the earth;*
  the time of singing has come,
and the voice of the turtledove

is heard in our land.
¹³The fig tree puts forth its figs,
   and the vines are in blossom;
   they give forth fragrance.
Arise, my love, my fair one,
   and come away."

SONG OF SONGS 3:6–11

⁶What is that coming up from the wilderness,
   like a column of smoke,
perfumed with myrrh and frankincense,
   with all the fragrant powders of the merchant?
⁷Look, it is the litter of Solomon!
Around it are sixty mighty men
   of the mighty men of Israel,
⁸all equipped with swords
   and expert in war,
each with his sword at his thigh
   because of alarms by night.
⁹King Solomon made himself a palanquin
   from the wood of Lebanon.
¹⁰He made its posts of silver,
   its back of gold, its seat of purple;
its interior was inlaid with love.
   Daughters of Jerusalem,
      ¹¹come out.
Look, O daughters of Zion,
   at King Solomon,
at the crown with which his mother crowned him
   on the day of his wedding,
   on the day of the gladness of his heart.

T he Song of Songs is a lyrical composition expressing desirous and devoted love. It reflects the lovers' emotions, longings, reminiscences,
expressions of mutual attraction, and declarations of fidelity. The
various elements of human love are freely blended: effusive joy, sensual pleasure, and heartfelt affection.

Undoubtedly this love poetry was reinterpreted based on the symbolism
of marriage and spousal love from the Torah and the prophets. So the Song
can be read from two different but closely connected viewpoints: that of human love and that of divine spousal love of which human love is the symbol.
Its liturgical use and allegorical interpretation influenced the transmission of
the text and its inclusion in the Scriptures.

The speaker draws attention to the coming of her beloved (2:8–9). He
approaches swiftly. Upon his arrival, he searches for her and calls her with
words that are urgent and tender: "Arise, my love, my fair one, and come
away" (2:10). There is mutual assertiveness and responsiveness: first, he
comes to her; now, she must go to him. She is urged to come forth, just as
the new life of spring has come forth. Nature is coming alive anew: flowers
cover the earth, the songs of birds are in the air, figs ripen on the vine, and
blossoms give forth fragrance. Sight, sound, scent, and taste are awakened in
the springtime, and desires are roused as the man calls the woman into love.
The fecundity of the natural world is compared with the fruitfulness that human love promises.

The Song continues with words that suggest a royal wedding. The groom
is a king, escorted by his men, each equipped "with his sword at his thigh"
(3:7–8). The sixty mighty men offer both honor and protection to the royal
figure. The king is transported in a covered litter, made of gold and silver, with
a seat of purple, borne by means of poles on the shoulders of men (3:9–10).
The daughters of Jerusalem are called upon to witness the crowning of the
king by the queen mother, who always had a prominent role in the gover-
nance of the royal sons of David (3:11). The crown is a symbol of royal power
as well as the traditional ornament of the bridegroom.

The Song of Songs has been interpreted in a variety of ways in the Jewish
and Christian traditions. The Jewish tradition understands these verses as a
symbolic description of the future wedding between God and the chosen
people. Much of the language describing the bridegroom is used elsewhere

in Scripture to describe God. Likewise, the language describing the bride is traditional vocabulary describing the land and temple of ancient Israel. The Song never actually describes the marriage and its consummation. Rather, the bride continues to wait for her divine lover. She cries for God to come over the mountains to Jerusalem, to come swiftly like a gazelle.

This interpretation contributed to Jewish messianic hope for a new marriage covenant. The Messiah will come like a bridegroom who will unite himself to them in an everlasting spousal bond. The Song resounds with a sense of paradise regained and even improved. There is not the slightest allusion to the disappointment that threatens all married couples, but it expresses that new creative moment, the perfect state of love, for which we all dream and long.

Reflection and discussion

- In what ways is genuine love like the changing seasons of the year?

- What is the role of longing in a spousal relationship? In what ways is this longing similar to life in covenant with God?

Prayer

Divine Beloved, you swiftly come to me, and you call me to arise and come forth to you. Plant within me a deep desire for you and a longing for your presence. Help me to seek you with all my heart and place my trust in you.

SUGGESTIONS FOR FACILITATORS, GROUP SESSION 3

1. Welcome group members and ask if there are any announcements anyone would like to make.

2. You may want to pray this prayer as a group:
   Redeeming God, for a moment you turned away from your people in your wrath, but with great compassion you have gathered them with your everlasting love. We know that your faithfulness will never end and your covenant will never be removed. Use our failures to draw us to yourself as we see your hand at work even in our adversities. Plant within us a deepening desire for your love as we experience your delight in us, as the bridegroom rejoices over the bride. As we gather to study your word in the Bible, inspire new hope within us, assure us of your presence, and guide us in your will.

3. Ask one or more of the following questions:
   - Which message of Scripture this week speaks most powerfully to you?
   - What is the most important lesson you learned through your study this week?

4. Discuss lessons 7 through 12. Choose one or more of the questions for reflection and discussion from each lesson to discuss as a group. You may want to ask group members which question was most challenging or helpful to them as you review each lesson.

5. Remember that there are no definitive answers for these discussion questions. The insights of group members will add to the understanding of all. None of these questions require an expert.

6. After talking about each lesson, instruct group members to complete lessons 13 through 18 on their own during the six days before the next group meeting. They should write out their own answers to the questions as preparation for next week's group discussion.

7. Ask the group if anyone is having any particular problems with the Bible study during the week. You may want to share advice and encouragement within the group.

8. Conclude by praying aloud together the prayer at the end of one of the lessons discussed. You may add to the prayer based on the sharing that has occurred in the group.

"The wedding guests cannot fast while the bridegroom is with them, can they? As long as they have the bridegroom with them, they cannot fast." MARK 2:19

The Bridegroom Is with Us

MARK 2:18–22 ¹⁸*Now John's disciples and the Pharisees were fasting; and people came and said to him, "Why do John's disciples and the disciples of the Pharisees fast, but your disciples do not fast?" ¹⁹Jesus said to them, "The wedding guests cannot fast while the bridegroom is with them, can they? As long as they have the bridegroom with them, they cannot fast. ²⁰The days will come when the bridegroom is taken away from them, and then they will fast on that day.*

²¹*"No one sews a piece of unshrunk cloth on an old cloak; otherwise, the patch pulls away from it, the new from the old, and a worse tear is made. ²²And no one puts new wine into old wineskins; otherwise, the wine will burst the skins, and the wine is lost, and so are the skins; but one puts new wine into fresh wineskins."*

In this gospel account, Jesus is challenged to explain why his disciples do not fast. The questioners expected Jesus, as a Jewish teacher, to hold his followers to the discipline of fasting. After all, the Pharisees practiced fasting and the followers of John the Baptist apparently imitated his ascetic lifestyle by fasting. But Jesus and his disciples, in contrast, failed to observe days of fasting.

Jesus responds to the challenge, as he often does, with a rhetorical question: "The wedding guests cannot fast while the bridegroom is with them, can they?" He uses the occasion to deepen the people's understanding of his identity and authority. In his counter-question, Jesus makes the point that he is "the bridegroom" and his followers are wedding guests (verse 19). In this joyful time, it is neither possible nor appropriate to fast.

This matrimonial imagery resonated with Jews who listened to Israel's prophets. The time of God's salvation was anticipated as a marriage feast, a time in which God would fully restore the nuptial bond between himself and his unfaithful people. The kingdom of God, now present in Jesus, is inaugurated like a joyful wedding banquet. In his Messiah, God is now bringing about that intimate communion with himself for which his people had been longing. Through the beginning of Jesus' ministry in Galilee, Israel's infidelities were about to be forgiven and the wedding covenant renewed once and for all.

But Jesus also hints forebodingly at a blot on the festivities—"when the bridegroom is taken away from them" (verse 20)—a veiled reference to his passion and death. Since Jesus will no longer be physically present among them, his disciples will rightly begin again the practice of fasting. This Christian fasting will be a way of anticipating and preparing for the full joy of the Messiah's wedding banquet, which the disciples will one day share.

The next two sayings of Jesus, about wearing new clothing and drinking wine, seem appropriate for the context of a wedding banquet (verses 21–22). The imagery of the unshrunken patch sown on an old cloak that results in a worse tear implies that old garments cannot simply be patched up. Rather, new garments are needed for this new age of God's salvation. Likewise, Jesus says that old wineskins break when new fermenting wine is stored in them. So new wineskins are necessary to hold the new wine of God's kingdom. The new clothing and new wineskins are metaphors for the radical renewal required of a person who chooses to live under God's reign. Jesus has not come merely to patch up God's people or to pour new life into brittle and unyielding lifestyles. He has come, rather, to transform God's people with the wedding feast of God's love.

Reflection and discussion

- Why is it neither possible nor appropriate for the disciples of Jesus to fast during his public ministry?

- What does the title of "bridegroom" imply about the ministry of Jesus?

- What old cloaks and old wineskins must I replace in order to celebrate God's wedding feast?

Prayer

Divine Bridegroom, you call your disciples to the joyful marriage banquet of your kingdom. Help me to respond to your invitation by replacing my old clothing with new so that you can fill my life with joy.

"For this reason a man shall leave his father and mother and be joined to his wife, and the two shall become one flesh." MARK 10:7

What God Has Joined, Let No One Separate

MARK 10:1–12 *¹He left that place and went to the region of Judea and beyond the Jordan. And crowds again gathered around him; and, as was his custom, he again taught them.*

²Some Pharisees came, and to test him they asked, "Is it lawful for a man to divorce his wife?" ³He answered them, "What did Moses command you?" ⁴They said, "Moses allowed a man to write a certificate of dismissal and to divorce her." ⁵But Jesus said to them, "Because of your hardness of heart he wrote this commandment for you. ⁶But from the beginning of creation, 'God made them male and female.' ⁷'For this reason a man shall leave his father and mother and be joined to his wife, ⁸and the two shall become one flesh.' So they are no longer two, but one flesh. ⁹Therefore what God has joined together, let no one separate."

¹⁰Then in the house the disciples asked him again about this matter. ¹¹He said to them, "Whoever divorces his wife and marries another commits adultery against her; ¹²and if she divorces her husband and marries another, she commits adultery."

For many today, marriage is a purely human institution, a historical invention, a man-made contract. As such, its character depends on the personal happiness of the spouses and whether they remain "in love." But Jesus and his followers, from ancient times until the present, have stood practically alone in teaching that true marriage is a permanent and indissoluble bond.

Divorce was widely accepted in Jewish society at the time of Jesus, although there was some debate about it among the leading rabbinical schools. So some Pharisees come to Jesus with a question designed to entrap him: "Is it lawful for a man to divorce his wife?" In the typical style of such discussion, Jesus responds with a counter-question, "What did Moses command you?"

The Pharisees answer Jesus by referring to a passage in Deuteronomy, the fifth book of Moses, which allows a man to write a certificate of dismissal "if she does not please him because he finds something objectionable about her" (Deut 24:1). There was, of course, much debate within Judaism over the meaning of "something objectionable" that would justify divorce. This passage, however, does not itself allow divorce; rather, it regulates what happens after a divorce. The provision offered some legal protection to a woman whose husband had repudiated her. A "certificate of dismissal" was a man's relinquishment of legal claims on his wife, freeing her from any obligation to him and allowing her to marry someone else.

Jesus explains that this provision of the law was necessary "because of your hardness of heart" (verse 5). This hardheartedness was attributed to God's people in the Old Testament to indicate a stubborn refusal to yield to God's ways. Jesus then focuses their attention on the first book of Moses and its creation accounts. Here is expressed God's original intention for marriage which is rooted in the divinely created nature of humanity before the effects of sin. "God made them male and female" and urged them to be fruitful and multiply (Gen 1:27–28). To express this covenant of love, a man leaves his parents and is joined to his wife, "and they become one flesh" (Gen 2:24). This spousal bond describes a personal and permanent union at the deepest level of their being.

Jesus solemnly declares what Genesis has already implied: "Therefore what God has joined together, let no one separate" (verse 9). With this teaching, Jesus confirms that God's original intention is the true standard for marriage. The long reign of sin has been broken with the coming of God's kingdom in Jesus, and with it comes the power to live what God intended for humanity from the beginning.

The disciples of Jesus want to make sure that he said what they think he said, so they question him away from the crowd. In ancient Israel a man was considered an adulterer when he had a sexual relationship with a married woman, in which case he was guilty of adultery against the husband of this woman, not his wife. But if a woman had a sexual relationship with another man, she was guilty of adultery against her husband. This reflected the view that a woman was in some sense the property of her husband. Jesus teaches, however, that what is adultery for one is adultery for the other, and that the sin of adultery is a sin against one's husband or wife. If a man dismisses his wife in favor of another, he commits adultery against his wife; and if a woman divorces her husband and marries another, she commits adultery against her husband. In this way, Jesus implicitly teaches that there is a basic equality between men and women in marriage and that each belongs to the other.

Jesus' teaching on the permanence of marriage was difficult for his first disciples, and it is difficult for the church today. Jesus calls husbands and wives to cultivate selfless love in order to maintain the commitment necessary for their marriage to endure. While the church continues to teach and uphold the ideal of Jesus, it also practices the compassion of Jesus in helping people who cannot live up to the ideal of marriage due to abuse, abandonment, or other factors. In carrying out the values of Jesus, the church seeks to help people prepare for marriage, to strengthen them in the struggles of marriage, and to support them in cases in which marriage cannot be maintained.

Reflection and discussion

- Fidelity in marriage was a characteristic of Christian life in contrast to the surrounding culture. Based on the Scriptures of Israel, why was this so important to Jesus?

- How does Jesus associate "hardness of heart" in this passage with the reign of sin?

- What is the justification of Jesus for his teaching on the permanence of the marriage covenant?

- How does this teaching encourage the church to help prepare couples for marriage and support them through the struggles of marriage?

Prayer

Divine Teacher, I find daily opportunities to put into practice your teachings on self-denial and commitment through the challenges of marriage and family life. Strengthen me in my promises to live out your design for human love and fidelity.

"In the resurrection whose wife will she be? For the seven had married her." MARK 12:23

The Question of Marriage in the Resurrection

MARK 12:18–27 *¹⁸Some Sadducees, who say there is no resurrection, came to him and asked him a question, saying, ¹⁹"Teacher, Moses wrote for us that 'if a man's brother dies, leaving a wife but no child, the man shall marry the widow and raise up children for his brother.' ²⁰There were seven brothers; the first married and, when he died, left no children; ²¹and the second married her and died, leaving no children; and the third likewise; ²²none of the seven left children. Last of all the woman herself died. ²³In the resurrection whose wife will she be? For the seven had married her."*

²⁴Jesus said to them, "Is not this the reason you are wrong, that you know neither the scriptures nor the power of God? ²⁵For when they rise from the dead, they neither marry nor are given in marriage, but are like angels in heaven. ²⁶And as for the dead being raised, have you not read in the book of Moses, in the story about the bush, how God said to him, 'I am the God of Abraham, the God of Isaac, and the God of Jacob'? ²⁷He is God not of the dead, but of the living; you are quite wrong."

Although the question asked of Jesus by the Sadducees was meant to trap Jesus, it touches on an issue that many ponder in each age: In what sense might a couple's marriage in this life continue in eternity? To his scheming opponents, Jesus gives an unambiguous answer as he tells them twice, "You are wrong" (verses 24, 27). But in suggesting to his opponents that they know "neither the scriptures not the power of God," Jesus makes them, and us, search for a deeper understanding of loving relationships and the resurrection.

Because the Sadducees did not believe in the resurrection of the dead, which the Pharisees and many other Jews affirmed, they devise an improbable scenario in order to point out the absurdity of the teaching. The test case of the woman who had successively married seven brothers is carefully crafted from the prescription in the Torah that if a man dies leaving a wife without any children, his brother should marry the wife and have children with her (Deut 25:5–6). The question of the Sadducees, "In the resurrection whose wife will she be?" is designed to confound Jesus and weaken his credibility as a teacher.

Jesus moves his listeners toward a less literal and more profound understanding of the resurrection of the dead. Some thought that resurrection was simply a return to conditions as we know them in this life. Resurrection in this sense is simply the resuscitation of corpses. In contrast, Jesus explains that the power of God not only restores the dead to life but gives them a new and completely transformed existence. Life in the resurrection will differ unimaginably from life as we know it now.

As for marriage in the resurrection, Jesus explains, "When they rise from the dead, they neither marry nor are given in marriage, but are like angels in heaven" (verse 25). Marriage is an earthly reality, intended to be fulfilled in this life, and not a relationship to be lived in the resurrected life. Risen men and women are glorified and live like angels. Sexual distinctions will no longer be linked to marriage, exclusive commitments, and childbearing. Notice that Jesus does not say that risen human beings become angels; rather, he says they become "like" angels. That is, they have a glorious and eternal existence like the angels.

The teaching of Jesus that marriage is a reality of the present age that is passing away does not deny that married couples will have a unique relationship in heaven. Those who were spouses on earth certainly retain memories of their love and continue to love one another forever. But earthly marriage, as good as it is, will give way to something far greater. Eternal union with God will infinitely surpass the earthly one-flesh union of husband and wife.

Jesus further teaches that our relationship with God remains through death and into the resurrection. Since "he is God not of the dead, but of the living" (verse 27), God remains in relationship with us through this life and into the next. When God was revealed to Moses as "the God of Abraham, the God of Isaac, and the God of Jacob," these patriarchs had long since died. Yet God has not forgotten his relationship with these heroes of faith; they and the rest of the righteous dead will enjoy his favor and experience his life. Indeed, the resurrection of Jesus and the future hope of all is based on the Scriptures and the power of God.

Reflection and discussion

- In what sense do the Sadducees understand neither the Scriptures nor the power of God?

- Why do you suppose there is no marriage in the resurrected life?

- Why can I not know or understand what life will be like in the resurrection? What do I wish I knew?

Prayer

Good Teacher, you confounded your challengers and taught those who listened to you to ponder more deeply. Help me to cherish the life and relationships you have given me, and to eagerly await the fullness of life you have planned for me forever.

"[The king] said to his slaves, 'The wedding is ready, but those invited were not worthy. Go therefore into the main streets, and invite everyone you find to the wedding banquet.'" MATT 22:8–9

The Royal Wedding Banquet

MATTHEW 22:1–14 *¹Once more Jesus spoke to them in parables, saying: ²"The kingdom of heaven may be compared to a king who gave a wedding banquet for his son. ³He sent his slaves to call those who had been invited to the wedding banquet, but they would not come. ⁴Again he sent other slaves, saying, 'Tell those who have been invited: Look, I have prepared my dinner, my oxen and my fat calves have been slaughtered, and everything is ready; come to the wedding banquet.'⁵But they made light of it and went away, one to his farm, another to his business, ⁶while the rest seized his slaves, mistreated them, and killed them. ⁷The king was enraged. He sent his troops, destroyed those murderers, and burned their city. ⁸Then he said to his slaves, 'The wedding is ready, but those invited were not worthy. ⁹Go therefore into the main streets, and invite everyone you find to the wedding banquet.'¹⁰Those slaves went out into the streets and gathered all whom they found, both good and bad; so the wedding hall was filled with guests.*

¹¹"But when the king came in to see the guests, he noticed a man there who was not wearing a wedding robe, ¹²and he said to him, 'Friend, how did you get in here without a wedding robe?' And he was speechless.¹³Then the king said to the attendants, 'Bind him hand and foot, and throw him into the outer darkness, where there will be weeping and gnashing of teeth.' ¹⁴For many are called, but few are chosen."

J esus' parable joins two previous comparisons: the Messiah as bridegroom and God's kingdom as a banquet. In this allegory, God is the king who gives the nuptial feast for the marriage of his royal son. Jesus is this son, the bridegroom of the wedding. The wedding banquet, as Jesus makes clear when he begins the parable, is a metaphor for the kingdom of heaven, the reign of God that Jesus has brought into the world. Jesus is the bridegroom of the royal wedding banquet, the messianic age of salvation to which all are invited.

The first part of the parable shows us invitations rejected (verses 3–6) and invitations accepted (verses 8–10). When the banquet is ready, the king sends his slaves out to summon those who had been previously invited to the royal feast. This first summons to the invited guests is simply rejected. When the king sends a second set of slaves with a more urgent message—"Everything is ready; come to the wedding banquet"—they make light of it, and some seize, mistreat, and kill the slaves. The first set of slaves represents the ancient prophets of Israel, who were so often rejected by God's people. The second set of slaves represent more recent prophets, apostles, and Christian missionaries—all those who communicate the message of God's kingdom coming in the person of Jesus Christ.

Those who were invited to the wedding banquet represent the leaders of Judaism who rejected Jesus and persecuted his disciples. The historical result of this infidelity on the part of Israel's leadership is the destruction of Jerusalem and its temple in AD 70 (verse 7). The king then sent his slaves out into the streets to bring in all who accepted the invitation. These represent all who received the gospel, tax collectors, sinners, people of the streets. These include Jews and eventually also Gentiles, so that God's kingdom is filled with banqueters (verses 9–10).

The second part of the parable makes the point that simply showing up at the wedding banquet is not sufficient; one must be prepared to enter the banquet as a full participant (verses 11–13). When the king entered and noticed a guest not wearing a "wedding robe," he had the guest thrown out of the banquet hall and into the darkness. The wedding robe seems to be a metaphor for repentance and the new lifestyle that the gospel invokes. The metaphor is similar to Paul's call for disciples to be clothed with Christ and with the characteristics of life in him (Gal 3:27; Col 3:12). The action of the king indicates that admittance into the banquet of God's reign is not a guarantee of staying there. Life in God's kingdom is a radically different life than one's former life in the "outer darkness."

The concluding saying—"For many are called, but few are chosen"—expresses a key message of the parable. Many are invited to receive the gospel and share in God's reign, but only those who respond to the gospel with repentance and a transformed life will be able to remain within the kingdom of God. The criteria for genuine discipleship is the same for all. Those who desire to share in the new life of God's reign must live a life of loving union with Jesus the Bridegroom.

Reflection and discussion

- What are the implications for Jesus' comparison of God's kingdom to a royal wedding banquet?

- Why do I sometimes feel unresponsive to my royal invitation to Christ's wedding banquet? What can I do this week to put on the proper "wedding robe" so that I may participate fully in the wedding banquet?

Prayer

Lord of the kingdom, thank you for the invitation to attend the wedding banquet of your Son. Help me to prepare myself well for the royal feast, with the proper attitude and clothing, so that I might enjoy the banquet and participate fully in the festivities you have planned for us.

"The bridegroom came, and those who were ready went with him into the wedding banquet; and the door was shut." MATT 25:10

Be Ready for the Bridegroom's Coming

MATTHEW 25:1–13 *[1]"Then the kingdom of heaven will be like this. Ten bridesmaids took their lamps and went to meet the bridegroom. [2]Five of them were foolish, and five were wise. [3]When the foolish took their lamps, they took no oil with them; [4]but the wise took flasks of oil with their lamps. [5]As the bridegroom was delayed, all of them became drowsy and slept. [6]But at midnight there was a shout, 'Look! Here is the bridegroom! Come out to meet him.' [7]Then all those bridesmaids got up and trimmed their lamps. [8]The foolish said to the wise, 'Give us some of your oil, for our lamps are going out.' [9]But the wise replied, 'No! there will not be enough for you and for us; you had better go to the dealers and buy some for yourselves.' [10]And while they went to buy it, the bridegroom came, and those who were ready went with him into the wedding banquet; and the door was shut. [11]Later the other bridesmaids came also, saying, 'Lord, lord, open to us.' [12]But he replied, 'Truly I tell you, I do not know you.' [13]Keep awake therefore, for you know neither the day nor the hour."*

The parable presents Jesus as the bridegroom who is coming to claim his bride as his own. The kingdom of God is presented again, as in the previous parable, as a wedding celebration. But here the parable is not about the invitation to the wedding, but about being prepared for it. The wise and the foolish bridesmaids are presented as positive and negative models of how to act in view of the delay in the coming of Christ.

The features of the parable are true to the customs of first-century Jewish weddings, insofar as we know them. In the weddings of Jesus' day, the wedding party would accompany the bridegroom from the house of the bride's family to his own house, where the feasting would begin. At the bride's house the groom would negotiate the terms of the marriage contract with the bride's father. If this discussion was prolonged or if a dispute arose, the groom could be delayed in coming.

The focus of the parable is on the ten bridesmaids who wait. Five of them are foolish because they expected the groom to arrive immediately and did not bring extra oil for their lamps. The other five are wise because they anticipated that the groom might be delayed and brought flasks of oil to replenish their lamps.

The bridegroom's delay in coming causes all the bridesmaids to get drowsy and fall asleep (verse 5). When the announcement is made that the groom's arrival is imminent, the wise maidens replenish their lamps with the oil while the foolish ones must go to the dealer to purchase more oil. At the coming of the bridegroom, the wise ones enter with him into the marriage festivities, but the foolish ones are shut out.

If the oil for the lamps has a particular allegorical meaning in the parable, it must be similar to the meaning of the wedding robe of the previous parable. The lack of a wedding robe and the lack of sufficient oil indicate a lack of preparedness. Perhaps the oil signifies trusting faith, enduring love, or good works that glorify God. Of course, like any good parable, it has numerous applications to a variety of situations.

The cry of the foolish bridesmaids, "Lord, lord, open to us," and the groom's answer, "Truly I tell you, I do not know you" (verses 11–12), is quite similar to the warning of Jesus at the end of the Sermon on the Mount. Those who cry out "Lord, Lord" but fail to do the will of God are met by the words of Jesus, "I never knew you; go away from me," and are unable to enter the kingdom (7:21–23).

Jesus' conclusion of the parable emphasizes its lesson: Constant alertness and preparedness is necessary because it is impossible to pinpoint the time of the Lord's coming. The parable is a warning to the church, which consists of both wise and foolish disciples. All must learn to remain vigilant, anticipating the Lord's coming while persevering in faithful service, proclaiming the kingdom to the world.

Reflection and discussion

- What are the similarities between this parable and that in Matthew 22:1–14? What is the primary difference?

- What is the oil that I must keep in steady supply so as to be ready to meet the Lord when he comes?

- Why is vigilance such an essential quality of the life of discipleship? How can I remain more watchful and ready?

Prayer

Divine Bridegroom, you have invited me to walk with you and enter the marriage celebration of the kingdom with you. Keep me strong in my faith, vigilant in hope, and faithful in my love for you.

"You are those who have stood by me in my trials; and I confer on you, just as my Father has conferred on me, a kingdom, so that you may eat and drink at my table in my kingdom." LUKE 22:28–30

The New Covenant in My Blood

LUKE 22:14–20, 28–30 ¹⁴*When the hour came, he took his place at the table, and the apostles with him.* ¹⁵*He said to them, "I have eagerly desired to eat this Passover with you before I suffer;* ¹⁶*for I tell you, I will not eat it until it is fulfilled in the kingdom of God."* ¹⁷*Then he took a cup, and after giving thanks he said, "Take this and divide it among yourselves;* ¹⁸*for I tell you that from now on I will not drink of the fruit of the vine until the kingdom of God comes."* ¹⁹*Then he took a loaf of bread, and when he had given thanks, he broke it and gave it to them, saying, "This is my body, which is given for you. Do this in remembrance of me."* ²⁰*And he did the same with the cup after supper, saying, "This cup that is poured out for you is the new covenant in my blood.*

²⁸*"You are those who have stood by me in my trials;* ²⁹*and I confer on you, just as my Father has conferred on me, a kingdom,* ³⁰*so that you may eat and drink at my table in my kingdom, and you will sit on thrones judging the twelve tribes of Israel."*

MATT 27:27–31 ²⁷*Then the soldiers of the governor took Jesus into the governor's headquarters, and they gathered the whole cohort around him.* ²⁸*They stripped him and put a scarlet robe on him,* ²⁹*and after twisting some thorns into a crown,* *they put it on his head. They put a reed in his right hand and knelt before him and mocked him, saying, "Hail, King of the Jews!"* ³⁰*They spat on him, and took the reed and struck him on the head.* ³¹*After mocking him, they stripped him of the robe and put his own clothes on him. Then they led him away to crucify him.*

I f Jesus is indeed the long-awaited bridegroom, when is his wedding banquet? From all indications, it must have certainly been his Last Supper. This final earthly meal with his disciples is described as a banquet of total, sacrificial love. His body is given and his blood is poured out for his disciples. The marriage is then consummated in his passion and cross.

As Jesus raised the cup of the Passover meal, his words focused on blood and covenant: "This cup that is poured out for you is the new covenant in my blood" (Luke 22:20). The words clearly alluded to "the blood of the covenant" between God and Israel made at Mount Sinai (Exod 24:8). This covenant, as the ancient Scriptures confirmed, was the nuptial event uniting God and his people. Now, at the Last Supper and through the Eucharist of Christ's church, Jesus unites himself with his church. Just as God wed himself to the twelve tribes of Israel at Mount Sinai through the blood of the old covenant, so now Jesus joins himself to the twelve disciples through the blood of the new covenant. Jesus the Bridegroom gives himself completely, in the sacrifice of his body and blood, for his church.

The loving sacrifice of Jesus for his bride began in the Upper Room and was consummated on the cross. The wine of his Passover became the blood of his sacrifice, the blood of the new covenant. Through the wine of Jesus' wedding banquet, God united his Son with his disciples forever, making them sharers in his body and blood.

As Jesus the Bridegroom traveled from the Last Supper to his crucifixion, he moved from his marriage feast to his bridal chamber where he would consummate his love for his bride. Of course, Jesus was not taken in a jubilant procession into a joyful chamber. Instead, he was taken away by soldiers to the marriage chamber of his passion.

The Jewish tradition maintains an amazing analogy between the union of God and Israel at the tabernacle in the wilderness and the union of the bridegroom and his bride in the tabernacle of the bridechamber (*chuppah,* in

Hebrew). In fact, the Jewish bridechamber, where the consummation of marriage took place, was made to look like the tabernacle. To this day, in orthodox Jewish weddings, the bride and groom make their marriage vows under a portable bridechamber, a canopy supported by four poles.

The tabernacle was the sacred place where God was united with his people in the wilderness. There Moses met with God, and sacrifice was offered to God each day. This tabernacle was the model for the temple in Jerusalem, the most sacred place on earth, where God continued to be united with Israel and sacrificial offerings renewed the covenant. Every marriage, then, was understood to be a reflection of God's union with Israel. The sacrificial offering of husband and wife to one another formed an image of God's covenanted relationship with his people.

The ancient theologians drew other parallels between the passion of Jesus and the wedding day of the Jewish bridegroom. They show how the gospel writers point beyond the historical facts of the crucifixion to the deeper reality of the Messiah's wedding day. For example, as the soldiers mocked Jesus, they put a scarlet robe on him and put a crown of thorns on his head (Matt 27:28–29). They were mocking his claims to be the Messiah, the royal son of God. This parallels the practice of the Jewish bridegroom who customarily wore a crown on his wedding day. As Solomon, the son of David, was crowned for his wedding, so every groom becomes a "king" for the day of his marriage (Song of Songs 3:11). Through his death and resurrection, Jesus was proclaimed king forever, ruling over the everlasting kingdom of God.

On the cross, Jesus consummated his marriage to his bride, not in pleasure but in pain. Through his blood, his sacrifice formed the nuptial covenant with his church. In the bridechamber of Calvary, Jesus united himself in a permanent and faithful marriage to his people, Jews and Gentiles, now and forever. This is the way it was expressed by St. Augustine, the fifth-century bishop of Hippo: "Like a bridegroom Christ…came to the marriage-bed of the cross, and there in mounting it, he consummated his marriage. And when he perceived the sighs of the creature, he lovingly gave himself up to the torment in place of his bride, and joined himself to her forever" (*Sermo Suppositus* 120).

Reflection and discussion

- In what sense is the Last Supper the wedding banquet of the Messiah?

- If Jewish weddings are performed under a canopy representing the bride-chamber (*chuppah*), what might be an appropriate setting for a Christian wedding?

- What is the significance for me that Jesus consummated his marriage covenant on the cross?

Prayer

King of all nations, you gave yourself completely to your church in the wedding banquet of your body and blood, and you formed the new covenant as our everlasting nuptial bond. Help me to respond faithfully to the love you have given to me.

SUGGESTIONS FOR FACILITATORS, GROUP SESSION 4

1. Welcome group members and ask if anyone has any questions, announcements, or requests.

2. You may want to pray this prayer as a group:
   Divine Bridegroom, you have given us the nuptial banquet of your body and blood as the sign of your new and everlasting covenant and as a foretaste of the eternal feast in your kingdom. Help us to cherish relationships you have given us so that we can faithfully live out your design for human love. Keep us strong in faith, vigilant in hope, and faithful in our love for you. May we eagerly await the fullness of life you have planned for us forever.

3. Ask one or more of the following questions:
   - What is the most difficult part of this study for you?
   - What insights stand out to you from the lessons this week?

4. Discuss lessons 13 through 18. Choose one or more of the questions for reflection and discussion from each lesson to discuss as a group. You may want to ask group members which question was most challenging or helpful to them as you review each lesson.

5. Keep the discussion moving, but allow time for the questions that provoke the most discussion. Encourage the group members to use "I" language in their responses.

6. After talking over each lesson, instruct group members to complete lessons 19 through 24 on their own during the six days before the next group meeting. They should write out their own answers to the questions as preparation for next week's session.

7. Ask the group what encouragement they need for the coming week. Ask the members to pray for the needs of one another during the week.

8. Conclude by praying aloud together the prayer at the end of one of the lessons discussed. You may choose to conclude the prayer by asking members to pray aloud any requests they may have.

"Everyone serves the good wine first, and then the inferior wine after the guests have become drunk. But you have kept the good wine until now." JOHN 2:10

The Marriage Feast at Cana

JOHN 2:1–11 *¹On the third day there was a wedding in Cana of Galilee, and the mother of Jesus was there. ²Jesus and his disciples had also been invited to the wedding. ³When the wine gave out, the mother of Jesus said to him, "They have no wine." ⁴And Jesus said to her, "Woman, what concern is that to you and to me? My hour has not yet come." ⁵His mother said to the servants, "Do whatever he tells you." ⁶Now standing there were six stone water jars for the Jewish rites of purification, each holding twenty or thirty gallons. ⁷Jesus said to them, "Fill the jars with water." And they filled them up to the brim. ⁸He said to them, "Now draw some out, and take it to the chief steward." So they took it. ⁹When the steward tasted the water that had become wine, and did not know where it came from (though the servants who had drawn the water knew), the steward called the bridegroom ¹⁰and said to him, "Everyone serves the good wine first, and then the inferior wine after the guests have become drunk. But you have kept the good wine until now." ¹¹Jesus did this, the first of his signs, in Cana of Galilee, and revealed his glory; and his disciples believed in him.*

Looking at the overall role of matrimonial imagery throughout the Bible, from creation in Genesis to the new creation in Revelation, we can better understand why the first public act of Jesus, "the first of his signs" to reveal his glory (verse 11), occurred at a Jewish wedding. This celebration of loving commitment, like all marriages, is a reflection of the spousal love of God for his people. Jesus' choice to begin his messianic mission in this context affirms the dignity of marriage and initiates his mission to bring God's nuptial desire to completion.

When the mother of Jesus said to him, "They have no wine," she is suggesting that he take on the role of the bridegroom, whose responsibility it is to provide the wine. But Jesus responds to her, "Woman, what concern is that to you and to me?" implying that it is not his responsibility to provide wine for the wedding feast (verse 4).

Jesus further states, "My hour has not yet come." As Jesus uses the word "hour" many more times in the gospel, the reader will realize that the "hour" of Jesus refers to his passion and death in which he will be exalted. But since this is the first time that Jesus uses the term "hour" in the gospels, its most natural understanding would be, "What concern is this to us? It's not my wedding," or "It's not yet the time for my wedding." This understanding amplifies the perception that his mother's request places him in the role of the bridegroom. Her refusal to accept no for an answer and Jesus' eventual positive response to her implied request points to his acceptance of the role of Israel's messianic bridegroom.

The original Jewish readers of John's gospel would have read this event in the context of Israel's ancient prophecy. Mary's report, "They have no wine," echoes the words of Isaiah, describing the people's desire for the wine of salvation: "The wine dries up, the vine languishes, all the merry-hearted sigh... No longer do they drink wine with singing...There is an outcry in the streets for lack of wine; all joy has reached its eventide; the gladness of the earth is banished" (Isa 24:7, 9, 11).

Israel's lack of wine is not the end of Isaiah's prophecy. These words lead to his famous prophecy of the messianic banquet: "On this mountain the Lord of hosts will make for all peoples a feast of rich food, a feast of well-aged wines, of rich food filled with marrow, of well-aged wines strained clear" (Isa 25:6). At this universal feast, the Lord will "swallow up death forever" and "wipe away tears from all faces." This is the wine for which all God's people long.

Thus, in the context of salvation history, the miracle of the wine at the wedding feast is Jesus' acceptance of his role as the long-awaited Messiah and as the bridegroom of God's people. By instructing the servants to fill six water jars to the brim and by changing the water to wine, Jesus demonstrates that Israel's hope for the abundant wine of the new age of salvation is beginning to be fulfilled in him. By providing wine of the highest quality for the wedding, Jesus shows that he is accepting the role of the messianic bridegroom, suggesting that all the prophecies of the divine bridegroom are pointed toward himself.

Jesus performs the miracle discreetly, not wanting to steal the spotlight and saving the family holding the banquet from any embarrassment. There is no indication that the guests understood what Jesus had done. When the steward tasted the water that had become wine, he called the bridegroom because he assumed the new wine had come from him. The steward praises him for having saved the good wine for last (verse 10). The irony is that Jesus has assumed the responsibility of the anonymous bridegroom in providing the wine for the feast. By taking the role of the bridegroom, Jesus begins to reveal the mystery of his divine identity.

Jesus' wedding gift of the wine is a prelude to the gift of his own life. The gospel anticipates the "hour" of Jesus, as the gospel moves from the wedding feast at Cana to the passion of Jesus in Jerusalem. His hour, which is his self-offering on the cross, is also the time of his wedding. When he is lifted up on the cross, he will give himself completely to his bride, the church.

Reflection and discussion

- In Judaism, wine is an expression of joyful celebration. Why would wine be associated in prophecy with the time of Israel's Messiah?

- What is the role of the Messiah's mother as the new age of salvation begins ?

- What does the abundance and quality of the new wine reveal about Jesus as the divine bridegroom?

- Why would Jesus have chosen a wedding banquet as the context for the first of his signs to reveal his glory?

Prayer

Lord of the age to come, you change water into wine and manifest yourself as the bridegroom of God's people. Help me to be grateful for the quantity and quality of the abundant life you have given me.

"He who has the bride is the bridegroom. The friend of the bridegroom, who stands and hears him, rejoices greatly at the bridegroom's voice. For this reason my joy has been fulfilled." JOHN 3:29

The Best Man Prepares the Way for the Bridegroom

JOHN 3:22–30 *²²After this Jesus and his disciples went into the Judean countryside, and he spent some time there with them and baptized. ²³John also was baptizing at Aenon near Salim because water was abundant there; and people kept coming and were being baptized ²⁴—John, of course, had not yet been thrown into prison. ²⁵Now a discussion about purification arose between John's disciples and a Jew. ²⁶They came to John and said to him, "Rabbi, the one who was with you across the Jordan, to whom you testified, here he is baptizing, and all are going to him." ²⁷John answered, "No one can receive anything except what has been given from heaven. ²⁸You yourselves are my witnesses that I said, 'I am not the Messiah, but I have been sent ahead of him.' ²⁹He who has the bride is the bridegroom. The friend of the bridegroom, who stands and hears him, rejoices greatly at the bridegroom's voice. For this reason my joy has been fulfilled. ³⁰He must increase, but I must decrease."*

In the transition to the new covenant, the role of John the Baptizer was essential. It seems that the ministries of John and Jesus overlapped for a period of time, each of them working in different areas. But when John's disciples told him that many of his own followers were going to Jesus, John clarifies his own place in God's plan in relationship to that of Jesus. His ministry of baptism with water is a preparation for the coming of the Messiah (verse 28).

John uses a matrimonial image to describe his relationship with Jesus: "He who has the bride is the bridegroom. The friend of the bridegroom, who stands and hears him, rejoices greatly at the bridegroom's voice" (verse 29). In relationship to Jesus the bridegroom, John is the "friend of the bridegroom" (*shoshbin*, in Hebrew). The role of the "friend of the bridegroom" is closest to the role of the best man of weddings today.

The role of this *shoshbin* was well known to first-century Judeans, and we know something about what was expected of this "best man" from rabbinical literature. The best man was chosen with much forethought by the bridegroom since he was responsible for all the preparations leading up to the wedding, almost as a wedding planner or organizer for the bridegroom. He would then function as the witness to the marriage.

With this image, John the Baptizer explained that he was the one who prepared the way for Jesus as the bridegroom. The greatest achievement for the best man would be that on the wedding day all the guests would be ready, waiting for the bridegroom to make his appearance. And on that day when he hears the voice of the groom, he rejoices because he knows that the groom has arrived and that his preparation is complete.

Although the focus of this scene is not on the bride but on the relation between the bridegroom and his best man, John emphasizes that "he who has the bride is the bridegroom" and not the best man. So when John receives the report that everyone is going to Jesus (verse 26), he knows that the bride and groom were finally coming together. His mission as preparer of the way has been completed in all its detail, so he is able to say, "My joy has been fulfilled."

As preparer of the way for the Messiah, John stood on the threshold between the old and the new covenants. He was the last of that long line of prophets that made Israel ready for the Messiah's coming. John had the privilege not only to prepare the way but to see him arrive in the flesh. Now all eyes are drawn away from the prophets and fixed upon Jesus the Christ. John's joy is fulfilled in the sense that he has seen the promises of Scripture becoming reality.

John's hearing and rejoicing at "the bridegroom's voice" echoes the words of the prophets who anticipated the age of the Messiah. In the divine promise of the messianic king in the line of David, Jeremiah speaks of the delight that will return to the cities of Judah and the streets of Jerusalem: "There shall once more be heard the voice of mirth and the voice of gladness, the voice of the bridegroom and the voice of the bride" (Jer 33:10–11). The delight of which Jeremiah speaks is the joy experienced by Israel's final prophet when he hears "the voice of the bridegroom."

This prophetic joy of the messianic age is reflected in every Jewish wedding. Toward the end of the ceremony, the Seven Blessings (*Sheva Berakhot*, in Hebrew) are recited under the canopy (*chuppah*). Here is the seventh blessing: "Blessed art You, O Lord, King of the universe, who has created joy and gladness, bridegroom and bride, mirth and exultation, pleasure and delight, love, harmony, peace, and friendship. Soon may there be heard in the cities of Judah and in the streets of Jerusalem, the voice of joy and gladness, the voice of the bridegroom and the voice of the bride, the jubilant voice of bridegrooms from their canopies, and of youths from their feasts of song. Blessed art Thou, O Lord, who causes the bridegroom to rejoice with the bride."

Following this seventh blessing, the bride and groom sip the wine. The blessings may be recited at table after the meal during the seven days of feasting following the wedding. This last of the marriage blessings is the only one in the form of a petition: "Soon may there be heard..." Here we reach the highest expression of delight, reciting multiple synonyms for the happiness of the bride and groom: joy, gladness, mirth, pleasure, delight, love, harmony, peace, and friendship.

Reflection and discussion

- Why does John the Baptizer long to hear the bridegroom's voice?

- Reflecting on the role of John the Baptizer in relationship to Jesus, St. Augustine said, "I am in the place of hearer; he, of speaker; I am the one who must be enlightened, he is the light; I am the ear, he is the word." In what ways must I be like John?

- In what ways does every Jewish wedding look toward the arrival of the Messiah in the age to come?

- How can reading the Bible help couples keep alive the joy and hope of Christian marriage?

Prayer

Messiah and Lord, the world still longs to hear the voice of the bridegroom and the voice of the bride. Bring us from the darkness of loss and longing, to the delight you have promised in the wedding banquet of your kingdom.

Then the woman left her water jar and went back to the city. She said to the people, "Come and see a man who told me everything I have ever done!" JOHN 4:28–29

A Samaritan Seeks
a True Husband

JOHN 4:3–30 *³[Jesus] left Judea and started back to Galilee. ⁴But he had to go through Samaria. ⁵So he came to a Samaritan city called Sychar, near the plot of ground that Jacob had given to his son Joseph. ⁶Jacob's well was there, and Jesus, tired out by his journey, was sitting by the well. It was about noon.*

⁷A Samaritan woman came to draw water, and Jesus said to her, "Give me a drink." ⁸(His disciples had gone to the city to buy food.) ⁹The Samaritan woman said to him, "How is it that you, a Jew, ask a drink of me, a woman of Samaria?" (Jews do not share things in common with Samaritans.) ¹⁰Jesus answered her, "If you knew the gift of God, and who it is that is saying to you, 'Give me a drink,' you would have asked him, and he would have given you living water." ¹¹The woman said to him, "Sir, you have no bucket, and the well is deep. Where do you get that living water? ¹²Are you greater than our ancestor Jacob, who gave us the well, and with his sons and his flocks drank from it?" ¹³Jesus said to her, "Everyone who drinks of this water will be thirsty again, ¹⁴but those who drink of the water that I will give them will never be thirsty. The water that I will give will become in them a spring of water gushing up to eternal life." ¹⁵The woman said to him, "Sir, give me this water, so that I may never be thirsty or have to keep coming here to draw water."

¹⁶Jesus said to her, "Go, call your husband, and come back." ¹⁷The woman answered him, "I have no husband." Jesus said to her, "You are right in saying, 'I have no husband'; ^{18}for you have had five husbands, and the one you have now is not your husband. What you have said is true!" ^{19}The woman said to him, "Sir, I see that you are a prophet. ^{20}Our ancestors worshiped on this mountain, but you say that the place where people must worship is in Jerusalem." ^{21}Jesus said to her, "Woman, believe me, the hour is coming when you will worship the Father neither on this mountain nor in Jerusalem. ^{22}You worship what you do not know; we worship what we know, for salvation is from the Jews. ^{23}But the hour is coming, and is now here, when the true worshipers will worship the Father in spirit and truth, for the Father seeks such as these to worship him. ^{24}God is spirit, and those who worship him must worship in spirit and truth." ^{25}The woman said to him, "I know that Messiah is coming" (who is called Christ). "When he comes, he will proclaim all things to us." ^{26}Jesus said to her, "I am he, the one who is speaking to you."

^{27}Just then his disciples came. They were astonished that he was speaking with a woman, but no one said, "What do you want?" or, "Why are you speaking with her?" ^{28}Then the woman left her water jar and went back to the city. She said to the people, ^{29}"Come and see a man who told me everything I have ever done! He cannot be the Messiah, can he?" ^{30}They left the city and were on their way to him.

After Jesus left Judea, where John the Baptizer had declared him to be the bridegroom, and was traveling northward toward Galilee, he encounters this Samaritan woman at Jacob's well. In the Hebrew Scriptures, the local well was not only a place where people met for conversation, it was also the place where Moses, Isaac, and Jacob met their spouses. Jacob met Rachel, his future bride, here at the well where Jesus was resting. Like Jesus, Jacob was a foreigner in a strange land. Like the Samaritan woman, Rachel came to the well at midday and encountered the stranger there. The setting and shape of the scene looks very much like a betrothal scene of old.

When Jesus asked the woman for a drink, she was surprised that Jesus would speak to her, since a Jewish man would ordinarily not speak to an unknown woman alone, and generally the Jews ignored if not detested Samaritans. Jesus did not plead ignorance; he was fully aware of the social rules and the Jewish intolerance of Samaritans. Yet he frequently broke social and religious boundaries for a higher good. Here Jesus uses his physical thirst as the occasion to address the deeper thirst of the Samaritan woman.

The symbol of the well, in the Song of Songs and other literature, represents the female element of a sexual relationship, whereas the spring or fountain represents the male element. Here the woman is identified with the well. As Jesus offers her living water, "a spring of water gushing up to eternal life," she begins to realize that he wants to extend to her the gift of a new and abundant life (verse 14). Through their "verbal intercourse" and her acceptance of the living water, she shares a spiritual intimacy and figurative marriage with Jesus the divine bridegroom.

Of course, Jesus, as a celibate Jew, was not looking for an ordinary wife, and the Samaritan woman, who had lived with five husbands, was not looking for another. Rather, the woman is being presented as a representative figure for the Samaritan people in relationship to Jesus, the messianic bridegroom. The symbolism is similar to that found in the prophet Hosea, where the prophet's wife represents God's people in relationship to their divine husband. For both the wife of Hosea and the Samaritan woman there is a remarkable parallel between the personal history of the woman and the religious history of her people. Just as the Samaritan woman has lived with five husbands, the Samaritan people have worshipped the deities of the foreign peoples who settled within the land.

As the woman admits that she has no husband, Jesus acknowledges that she is correct, for she has had five husbands, and the man with her now is not her husband (verses 17–18). While this might describe a tragic marital history, there is a figurative level to this scene in that the woman represents her people. The book of 2 Kings describes the resettlement of Samaria after the Assyrian conquest. People from five foreign nations settled there and mixed with the remaining people of Israel. Each of these peoples brought their own gods and religious practices, which compromised the covenant of God with Israel (2 Kings 17:24, 29–34). If the five husbands symbolized Samaria's relationship with these five idolatrous peoples, then the sixth, or present liaison, would be the Samaritans' infidelity to God by their worship on Mount Gerazim.

This figurative interpretation seems valid in light of the Samaritan woman's response to Jesus, which has nothing to do with marriage but is concerned with the correct place for worshiping God. The Samaritans considered Mount Gerazim as the proper place for sacrifice, while the Jews held Jerusalem to be the only suitable place (verse 20). Jesus replies that the place of worship will be relatively unimportant in the age of the Messiah. The new temple for all people will be the body of the Risen Lord, in which believers will worship in spirit and in truth (verse 24).

When the disciples of Jesus return, they are astonished that he is speaking with a Samaritan woman at Jacob's well (verse 27). They knew the many implications of such an encounter. Yet, while the men were astonished, this astonishing woman was going forth to witness to Jesus among her own people (verses 28–29). Her evangelizing style is invitational. She encourages others to "come and see" what she herself has experienced in Jesus. Her faith is still tentative and she is full of questions: "He cannot be the Messiah, can he?" By inviting others to share in her searching, she becomes the first missionary to the Samaritans, and they do indeed come and see: "They left the city and were on their way to him" (verse 30).

Reflection and discussion

- What indicates that the gospel writer wants the reader to interpret this scene as a symbolic marriage between Jesus the bridegroom and the woman of Samaria?

- Why was it necessary for the Samaritans to acknowledge their infidelity before committing their lives to Jesus, the messianic bridegroom?

Prayer

Savior of the world, you are the source of living water and the bridegroom of all peoples. Open my heart with a deep thirst for the new life you offer me. Quench my thirst with your presence and the gift of your Spirit.

Mary took a pound of costly perfume made of pure nard, anointed Jesus' feet, and wiped them with her hair. The house was filled with the fragrance of the perfume. JOHN 12:3

The Loving Intimacy of Mary of Bethany

JOHN 11:1–3, 31–36 *¹Now a certain man was ill, Lazarus of Bethany, the village of Mary and her sister Martha. ²Mary was the one who anointed the Lord with perfume and wiped his feet with her hair; her brother Lazarus was ill. ³So the sisters sent a message to Jesus, "Lord, he whom you love is ill."*

³¹The Jews who were with her in the house, consoling her, saw Mary get up quickly and go out. They followed her because they thought that she was going to the tomb to weep there. ³²When Mary came where Jesus was and saw him, she knelt at his feet and said to him, "Lord, if you had been here, my brother would not have died." ³³When Jesus saw her weeping, and the Jews who came with her also weeping, he was greatly disturbed in spirit and deeply moved. ³⁴He said, "Where have you laid him?" They said to him, "Lord, come and see." ³⁵Jesus began to weep. ³⁶So the Jews said, "See how he loved him!"

JOHN 12:1–7 *¹Six days before the Passover Jesus came to Bethany, the home of Lazarus, whom he had raised from the dead. ²There they gave a dinner for him. Martha served, and Lazarus was one of those at the table with him. ³Mary took a pound of costly perfume made of pure nard, anointed Jesus' feet, and wiped them with her hair. The house was filled with the fragrance of the perfume. ⁴But Judas*

Iscariot, one of his disciples (the one who was about to betray him), said, ⁵"Why was this perfume not sold for three hundred denarii and the money given to the poor?" ⁶(He said this not because he cared about the poor, but because he was a thief; he kept the common purse and used to steal what was put into it.) ⁷Jesus said, "Leave her alone. She bought it so that she might keep it for the day of my burial."

I n the previous chapters of John's gospel, Jesus has been portrayed as the messianic bridegroom at the wedding in Cana and by John the Baptizer. Further, the Samaritan woman has been portrayed as the representative figure for the Samaritan people and the figurative bride of the messianic bridegroom. Similarly, in this scene, Mary of Bethany is portrayed as the representative figure of the Jews and the figurative bride of the messianic bridegroom.

At the beginning of the account of Lazarus' death and raising by Jesus, the evangelist described Mary as "the one who anointed the Lord with perfume and wiped his feet with her hair" (11:2). As the account continues, Mary is continually associated with "the Jews" and emotionally bonded to them (11:31, 33). They follow her to the tomb, and they weep with her. This grieving of Mary and the Jews who were with her causes Jesus to weep also (11:35). The depth of the emotional response of Mary and the Jewish community associated with her moves Jesus to both tears and action.

After Jesus raised Lazarus to life, the Jews "who had come with Mary" and seen the miracle put their faith in Jesus (11:45). They echo the faith of Mary that she has expressed throughout the account. This physical, emotional, and spiritual union of Mary with the Jewish people is similar to the bond of the woman at the well with the Samaritan people. Like her, Mary facilitates some of her people to believe in Jesus. In this way, Mary too becomes a figurative bride of the messianic bridegroom. The woman of Samaria represents the Samaritans who come to believe in Jesus, and Mary of Bethany represents the Jews who come to believe in Jesus.

When Mary first encountered Jesus after the tragedy of her brother's death, she fell at the feet of Jesus and wept. Later when Jesus came to the family's home for dinner, Mary again approached the feet of Jesus, this time anointing them with perfume and wiping them with her hair (12:3). The dinner was most probably eaten in customary style, with Jesus and the guests reclining on their side with their feet pointing away from the food. As Martha served the meal, Mary sat at the feet of Jesus to perform the anointing. Mary's gesture suggests tender and loving intimacy. The costliness of the perfume expresses the extravagance of her love for Jesus.

The preciousness of the perfume made with pure nard dictated that it be applied a few drops at a time in normal use. To use a pound at once seemed, in the eyes of many, irrational and excessive. As she poured out the nard and wiped the feet of Jesus with her hair, Mary filled the house with the fragrance (12:3). There may be an allusion here to the Song of Songs: "While the king is on his couch, my nard gave forth its fragrance" (Song 1:12). This ancient song of the love between God and his people echoes through the gospel text to express the love of Mary for her royal bridegroom. The committed love of Mary for Jesus fills the whole scene with the fragrance of devotion.

The scene juxtaposes Mary's genuine love with Judas' hypocrisy and self-interest. The extravagant scene represents in miniature what Jesus will do in the final days of his life. His love is lavish. He will pour out his lifeblood to anoint his beloved ones with grace. His actions seem excessive to many, but the fragrance of his divine love fills the whole world. Mary's lavish anointing is a preview of Christ's self-giving and alerts us to the fact that the passion of Jesus is more about loving than about suffering. The love of Jesus leads to the most significant and beautiful act in all of history as he pours out his all for us.

Reflection and discussion

- In what ways does the gospel writer associate Mary of Bethany physically, emotionally, and spiritually with Jewish believers?

- In what ways are the Samaritan woman and Mary of Bethany shown to be symbolic brides of Jesus the bridegroom?

- How is the extravagant love of Mary a preview for the lavish self-giving of Jesus?

- Why is my love for Jesus so often measured and conditional? How can my love become more lavish and abundant?

Prayer
Generous Lord, I want to love you with my whole mind, heart, will, and strength. Keep me from being too calculating in my words and deeds, and help me to act with greater extravagance in relationship to you.

**When Jesus had received the wine, he said, "It is finished."
Then he bowed his head and gave up his spirit.** JOHN 19:30

The Side of Jesus Is Pierced

JOHN 19:25–37 ²⁵*Meanwhile, standing near the cross of Jesus were his mother, and his mother's sister, Mary the wife of Clopas, and Mary Magdalene. ²⁶When Jesus saw his mother and the disciple whom he loved standing beside her, he said to his mother, "Woman, here is your son." ²⁷Then he said to the disciple, "Here is your mother." And from that hour the disciple took her into his own home.*

²⁸*After this, when Jesus knew that all was now finished, he said (in order to fulfill the scripture), "I am thirsty." ²⁹A jar full of sour wine was standing there. So they put a sponge full of the wine on a branch of hyssop and held it to his mouth. ³⁰When Jesus had received the wine, he said, "It is finished." Then he bowed his head and gave up his spirit.*

³¹*Since it was the day of Preparation, the Jews did not want the bodies left on the cross during the sabbath, especially because that sabbath was a day of great solemnity. So they asked Pilate to have the legs of the crucified men broken and the bodies removed. ³²Then the soldiers came and broke the legs of the first and of the other who had been crucified with him. ³³But when they came to Jesus and saw that he was already dead, they did not break his legs. ³⁴Instead, one of the soldiers pierced his side with a spear, and at once blood and water came out. ³⁵(He who saw this has testified so that you also may believe. His testimony is true, and he knows that he tells the truth.) ³⁶These things occurred so that the scripture might be fulfilled, "None of his bones shall be broken." ³⁷And again another passage of scripture says, "They will look on the one whom they have pierced."*

A t the wedding feast in Cana, Jesus responded to his mother, "My hour has not yet come." In the immediate context of the banquet, these words of Jesus could be interpreted as "It's not yet the time for my wedding." The gospel, then, anticipates the "hour" of Jesus, as the gospel moves from the wedding feast at Cana to the passion of Jesus in Jerusalem. As the passion of Jesus begins at the Last Supper, the evangelist writes, "Jesus knew that his hour had come to depart from this world and go to the Father. Having loved his own who were in the world, he loved them to the end" (13:1). His hour, which leads to his self-offering on the cross, is also the time of his wedding as the messianic bridegroom, the expression of this love "to the end." As he is lifted up on the cross, he gives himself completely to his bride, the church.

The mother of Jesus, who initiated the public ministry of Jesus at Cana, appears once again at the climactic moment of Jesus' death. The evangelist lists her first among three other women standing near the cross of Jesus. The evangelist also states that the beloved disciple is standing beside the mother of Jesus. This "disciple whom he loved" is not only a historical disciple in the ministry of Jesus but also a representational figure throughout the gospel. He is the model disciple and the ideal witness to Jesus. Jesus gives the beloved disciple to his mother as her son, and Jesus also gives his mother to the beloved disciple as his mother. In this mutual exchange, Jesus is clearly doing more than just providing for the care of his grieving mother. She is entrusted by Jesus with the spiritual motherhood of his church.

Throughout the passion account, Jesus has been presented as a king. Jesus is mocked as a king with a purple robe and crown of thorns; then Pilate presents him to the crowd with the words, "Here is your King!" Because he is Israel's Messiah, Jesus is truly King. But, according to his response to Pilate, his kingdom is "not from this world." In the royal line of King David, the mother of the king held an important role during his reign. She sat on a throne to the right of her son, exercised the position of queen mother, and served as an advocate for the people (1 Kgs 2:17). At the king's wedding, the queen mother stood at his right hand (Ps 45:9). Thus, the mother of Jesus, though not a queen in this world, is truly the queen mother in Christ's kingdom, exercising maternal care over his church.

Although Jesus had declared to his mother at Cana that his hour had not yet come for him to give the wine of salvation, he drinks the wine of Calvary on the cross in the presence of his mother (verses 29–30). After drinking this wine, the bridegroom declared, "It is finished," and gives over his life. The hour for the Messiah's self-gift—his love to the end and the consummation of the new and everlasting marriage covenant—had arrived in his sacrificial outpouring on the cross.

The final image of Jesus on the cross depicts the side of Jesus being pierced by the soldier's spear and the blood and water flowing out (verse 34). The evangelist's emphasis on the eyewitness testimony, its precise detail, and its fulfillment of Scripture heightens the scene's significance (verses 35–37). The scene is carefully described for the faith of future generations, "so that you also may believe" in the unseen significance of the moment. Throughout the Scriptures, both water and blood represent life. Blood is the sacred principle of life, and blood poured out sacrificially sealed covenants and atoned for sins. Water is life's most basic necessity, and living water represents new life in God's Spirit. The pierced side of Jesus declares that the effects of the cross do not end with the Messiah's death, but spring forth in a flow of new life.

The scene of the flowing blood and water evokes the image of giving birth. It also recalls the creation scene in which God fashions the woman from the side of the man (Gen 2:21–22). As St. Augustine said, "The church the Lord's Bride was created from the Lord's side, as Eve was created from the side of Adam" (Augustine, *Exposition on Psalm 127:4*). Just as God "caused a deep sleep to fall upon the man" so that God could form the woman from the man's side, so too Jesus fell into the sleep of death, and blood and water flowed from his side, giving birth to his church. And just as God's creation of the first bride from the side of Adam is the foundation for marriage (Gen 2:23–24; Mark 10:6–9), so too the flow of blood and water from the side of Jesus is the eternal witness to the marriage of Christ and his church.

Reflection and discussion

- How does Jesus form a new family of faith as he gives his life on the cross?

- In what ways does the role of the queen mother in Israel's monarchy help me to understand the role of the mother of Jesus for his church?

- In what sense can it be said that the church, the bride of Christ, is formed from his side?

Prayer

Son of God and Son of Mary, from your death on the cross, you gave your church the blood of the new covenant and the water of eternal life. Through the grace of your word and sacraments, may your kingdom come on earth as it is in heaven.

Early on the first day of the week, while it was still dark, Mary Magdalene came to the tomb and saw that the stone had been removed from the tomb. JOHN 20:1

Mary Magdalene Desires to Hold the Risen Lord

JOHN 20:11–18 *¹¹Mary [Magdalene] stood weeping outside the tomb. As she wept, she bent over to look into the tomb; ¹²and she saw two angels in white, sitting where the body of Jesus had been lying, one at the head and the other at the feet. ¹³They said to her, "Woman, why are you weeping?" She said to them, "They have taken away my Lord, and I do not know where they have laid him." ¹⁴When she had said this, she turned around and saw Jesus standing there, but she did not know that it was Jesus. ¹⁵Jesus said to her, "Woman, why are you weeping? Whom are you looking for?" Supposing him to be the gardener, she said to him, "Sir, if you have carried him away, tell me where you have laid him, and I will take him away." ¹⁶Jesus said to her, "Mary!" She turned and said to him in Hebrew, "Rabbouni!" (which means Teacher). ¹⁷Jesus said to her, "Do not hold on to me, because I have not yet ascended to the Father. But go to my brothers and say to them, 'I am ascending to my Father and your Father, to my God and your God.'" ¹⁸Mary Magdalene went and announced to the disciples, "I have seen the Lord"; and she told them that he had said these things to her.*

Mary Magdalene is the only woman described in all four gospels as a witness both to the cross and the resurrection of Jesus. In John's gospel, she comes alone to the tomb in the morning darkness of the week's first day. In the other gospels, she comes to the tomb with other women with the express purpose of anointing his body. But in this gospel, Jesus' body had already been properly prepared for burial by Joseph of Arimathea and Nicodemus (19:38–42). Here, Mary seems to search out the tomb because of the pain of being separated from him. As a woman who dearly loves Jesus, Mary is overwhelmed with her loss and cries tears of grief (verses 11, 13, 15). She hopes that visiting the tomb and seeing his body will fend off the ache of separation and express a love that survives death.

When the risen Jesus asks her why she is weeping and for whom she is looking, she sees him but does not realize it is Jesus. She continues to insist that someone has taken away the body of Jesus. Only when he calls her by name, "Mary," does she recognize him (verse 16). The calling of her name enables Mary to give Jesus her full attention and to create the personal bond with him that establishes faith.

Seeing Jesus now alive, Mary Magdalene instinctively embraces him. But Jesus gently asks her not to "hold on" to him because he has not yet returned to the Father (verse 17). She is trying to hold Jesus as if he were still in the flesh, but Jesus insists that she not attempt to reestablish the same relationship she once had with him. Mary and the other disciples must learn a new way of knowing Jesus. His permanent presence with them will come only with the gift of the Spirit as he ascends to the Father. Mary and all who love Jesus will then be able to embrace him in a new and much better way.

John's gospel emphasizes that the place of Jesus' burial and resurrection is a garden (19:41). Before Mary was able to identify Jesus, she presumed him to be the gardener. These garden references echo the scenes of the original couple in the garden and the joy of their first encounter. Even more significantly, the scene alludes to the Song of Songs in which the bride urgently searches for her spouse in the early hours of dawn: "Upon my bed at night I sought him whom my soul loves; I sought him and found him not; I called him, but he gave no answer. 'I will rise now and go about the city, in the streets and in the squares; I will seek him whom my soul loves.' I sought him, but found him not" (Song 3:1–2). After passing the sentinels and inquiring about her beloved, she finally finds him: "I held him, and would not let him go" (Song 3:4). Although the woman's search seems to be a dream quest in the Song, it poetically expresses Mary's anxiety to find Jesus in the early hours and her desire to cling to him and not let him go.

The tenderness of the gospel scene and its allusions to spousal love in other literature point to Mary Magdalene as the final figurative bride, like the Samaritan woman and Mary of Bethany before her. Because the theme of Jesus as the messianic bridegroom seems to run throughout the gospel, Mary Magdalene functions as a representative of the broad faith community called to discipleship, just as the woman at the well represents the Samaritan people and Mary of Bethany represents the Jews who believe in Jesus.

After the encounter between Mary Magdalene and Jesus, they do not live together happily ever after. Rather than embrace his bride, Jesus gives her an evangelizing mission to the other disciples. After all (despite the claims of heretical writings in later centuries), they are not literally spouses and theirs is not an earthly marriage. Jesus remains a celibate Jew even in his glorious state, and Mary becomes a significant female disciple in the early church. But in John's gospel, Mary represents the committed and intimate bond that Jesus desires to deepen with his community of disciples.

As the first to announce the resurrection to others, Mary Magdalene proclaims, "I have seen the Lord" (verse 18). She is referring to an experience far deeper and more real than simply a visual sighting. Her experience is one of loving recognition, a deeply personal and mystical encounter. Mary has moved from the darkness to the light of faith. She has seen Jesus as Lord, and she cannot help but become the messenger of that good news to others.

Reflection and discussion

- How might visiting the tomb of Jesus help relieve her grief?

- What aspects of the encounter between Jesus and Mary Magdalene suggest a spousal relationship?

- What is the meaning of Mary Magdalene's proclamation, "I have seen the Lord"?

- The church's belief in the resurrection of Jesus originates with the witness of Mary Magdalene. In what way can she be a model of faith for me?

Prayer

Risen Lord, you have called me by name to experience an intimate union of life with you. Turn my weeping to joy, my despair to hope, and my disbelief to the fullness of confident trust.

SUGGESTIONS FOR FACILITATORS, GROUP SESSION 5

1. Welcome group members and ask if anyone has any questions, announcements, or requests.

2. You may want to pray this prayer as a group:

   Messiah and Lord, you began to manifest yourself as the bridegroom of God's people at the wedding of Cana. Enlighten us to see ourselves in the Samaritan woman, Mary of Bethany, and Mary Magdalene in their spousal relationship to you. Bring us to a deeper intimacy of life with you so that we may love you with our whole mind, heart, will, and strength. Lead us from our present longings to the delight you have promised in the wedding banquet of your kingdom.

3. Ask one or more of the following questions:
   - What most intrigued you from this week's study?
   - How can this study of God's spousal love strengthen marriages?

4. Discuss lessons 19 through 24. Choose one or more of the questions for reflection and discussion from each lesson to talk over as a group.

5. Ask the group members to name one thing they have most appreciated about the way the group has worked during this Bible study. Ask group members to discuss any changes they might suggest in the way the group works in future studies.

6. Invite group members to complete lessons 25 through 30 on their own during the six days before the next meeting. They should write out their own answers to the questions as preparation for next week's session.

7. Discuss ways in which an understanding of God's spousal love could be helpful for the pastoral ministry within your community.

8. Conclude by praying aloud together the prayer at the end of one of the lessons discussed. You may want to conclude the prayer by asking members to voice prayers of thanksgiving.

If God is for us, who is against us? He who did not withhold
his own Son, but gave him up for all of us, will he not with him
also give us everything else? ROM 8:31–32

Nothing Can Separate Us
from the Love of God

ROMANS 8:28–39 *²⁸We know that all things work together for good for those
who love God, who are called according to his purpose. ²⁹For those whom he fore-
knew he also predestined to be conformed to the image of his Son, in order that he
might be the firstborn within a large family. ³⁰And those whom he predestined he
also called; and those whom he called he also justified; and those whom he justified
he also glorified.*

*³¹What then are we to say about these things? If God is for us, who is against
us? ³²He who did not withhold his own Son, but gave him up for all of us, will he
not with him also give us everything else? ³³Who will bring any charge against
God's elect? It is God who justifies. ³⁴Who is to condemn? It is Christ Jesus, who
died, yes, who was raised, who is at the right hand of God, who indeed intercedes
for us. ³⁵Who will separate us from the love of Christ? Will hardship, or distress, or
persecution, or famine, or nakedness, or peril, or sword? ³⁶As it is written,*

"For your sake we are being killed all day long;
we are accounted as sheep to be slaughtered."

*³⁷No, in all these things we are more than conquerors through him who loved
us. ³⁸For I am convinced that neither death, nor life, nor angels, nor rulers, nor things
present, nor things to come, nor powers, ³⁹nor height, nor depth, nor anything else in
all creation, will be able to separate us from the love of God in Christ Jesus our Lord.*

The spousal love of God, as proclaimed throughout the Scriptures, leads Paul in this letter to praise God's inseparable love for us made visible in Jesus Christ. God's spousal love is also a parental love, welcoming us into a large family, with Jesus, the Son of God, as the firstborn among many siblings (verse 29). Paul assures us that "all things work together for good" for those whose lives are enveloped in this divine love (verse 28). Whether it is health or sickness, joy or sorrow, comfort or suffering, God makes everything eventually work out for the good. Often, however, we can see the good only in hindsight, as we look back upon our lives. God's saving plan takes us through many stages in our life's journey: God chooses us, sets us apart, calls us, justifies us, all directed toward the goal of sharing in God's glory (verse 30).

We can have absolute confidence in our future because we know it is in the hands of our all-powerful and all-loving God, not our own. Nothing can disturb that unshakable hope. "God is for us" (verse 31)—this is the essence of the gospel Paul proclaims. As with all great truths, its articulation is disarmingly simple. Paul eloquently praises God for his absolute faithfulness verified for the world in the person of Jesus Christ, "who died, ... who was raised, who is at the right hand of God, who indeed intercedes for us" (verse 34). As the one who died, Jesus redeemed humanity from sin and judgment; as the one who was raised, he assures us of victory over death and the gift of eternal life. As the one at the right hand of God, Jesus reigns as Lord in power and glory. As the one who intercedes for us, the enthroned Lord exercises his authority on our behalf. Jesus assures us that God is for us, not only in his sacrificial love on the cross but also now in his sustaining love as our glorious Lord.

This faithfulness of God's love is extolled through a volley of rhetorical questions (verses 31–35). The questions answer themselves and praise the God who is always with us and for us. With God on our side, the forces that are marshaled against us cannot prevail. Since God even gave up his Son for our sake, paying the highest possible price, we can certainly trust God to give us everything we could possibly need (verse 32). Because the only one of any significance who could bring a charge against us or condemn us is the one who has done everything for us, then truly we have nothing to be afraid of (verses 33–34). Since God has proven his love for us absolutely, we need not worry about any opposition. Not even the greatest dangers and most painful experiences that humans could undergo can separate us from God's love (verse 35).

In a final crescendo, Paul tries to establish our trust beyond a shadow of a doubt. Since God has made us "more than conquerors" (verse 37), having conquered the greatest of all enemies through Christ, we can live with confident assurance that God is for us. Not even the strongest forces of the universe—earthly or cosmic, natural or supernatural, present or future—can separate us from God's love (verses 38–39). Paul uses all the fiercest terms he can imagine to show how ineradicable is the divine love that he has come to know through Jesus Christ.

Reflection and discussion

- What is one way I have seen God make suffering or sorrow work out for the good?

- Spend a few moments reflecting on verses 38–39. What are the feelings that remain with me?

Prayer

Lord Jesus Christ, through your death, resurrection, and glorious reign you have demonstrated the trustworthiness and fidelity of God's love. In the face of life's trials, sorrows, and suffering, assure me that nothing can separate me from that love.

I feel a divine jealousy for you, for I promised you in marriage to one husband, to present you as a chaste virgin to Christ. 2 COR 11:2

Paul Has Betrothed the Community to Christ

2 CORINTHIANS 11:1–4 *¹I wish you would bear with me in a little foolishness. Do bear with me! ²I feel a divine jealousy for you, for I promised you in marriage to one husband, to present you as a chaste virgin to Christ. ³But I am afraid that as the serpent deceived Eve by its cunning, your thoughts will be led astray from a sincere and pure devotion to Christ. ⁴For if someone comes and proclaims another Jesus than the one we proclaimed, or if you receive a different spirit from the one you received, or a different gospel from the one you accepted, you submit to it readily enough.*

In this section of Paul's correspondence with the church in Corinth, he expresses a sense of urgency for the spiritual welfare of the community, so much so that he asks them to bear with him in a bit of "foolishness." Although we cannot fully identify all the issues with which Paul was dealing, he is warning the community about false teachers, those who impart a different message about Jesus than the one taught by himself. Paul explains in a later text that his "foolishness" is a kind of boasting, a focus on himself and his own qualities of leadership that might sound like bragging. But Paul knows that he must take this risk of defending himself by boasting because the strategies of the false teachers have forced it upon him.

In explaining the reasons for his urgency, Paul admits his "jealousy" (verse 2). But he adds that his jealousy for the community is a "divine jealousy." The Greek phrase is literally "I am jealous about you with a jealousy from God." Human jealousy is often selfish, but divine jealousy is an intense affection for the other that is oriented toward the good of the other. In fact, in the Old Testament, God is described as "jealous" when making his covenant with Israel (Exod 20:5; 34:14). Similarly, Paul shares God's jealousy toward the church.

Paul uses the nuptial imagery found throughout Scripture of the divine Spouse committed in marriage to God's people. Here he speaks of Christ as the divine husband and the church as a chaste virgin betrothed to him. Paul designates himself as the one who arranged for the betrothal and the one who will present the bride to her husband for the marriage. Paul's role in this metaphor has been described as a matchmaker, wedding broker, friend of the bridegroom, best man, or the father of the bride. The latter seems to fit the image best, especially since Paul had already described himself as the spiritual father of the Corinthian church: "I became your father through the gospel" (1 Cor 4:15). During the betrothal period, it was the father's responsibility to watch over and protect his daughter. During this time of their betrothal, between their Christian conversion and Christ's glorious return, Paul was obliged to guard and defend her from harm. The reason for Paul's urgency is his solemn commitment to prepare the church for Christ and to keep her faith intact; as he says, "I promised you in marriage to one husband."

The false teachers present a danger to the community, seducing the Corinthian believers from the purity of the message proclaimed by Paul. He compares their deception to that of the serpent in the garden who tricked the original married couple (verse 3). Just as Eve was deceived by false ideas and twisted logic, the church is in danger of being led astray from its "sincere and pure devotion to Christ." The Genesis account of the first couple shows how this deception leads to both vertical and horizontal disorder. It leads to a rupture in the relationship between God and humanity, and it wreaks havoc on the committed connection between spouses.

Finally, Paul justifies his urgency in that the Corinthians are submitting to a different Jesus than the one Paul proclaimed; thus, they are receiving a "different spirit" and a "different gospel" (verse 4). The true Jesus, the Holy Spirit, and the gospel are inseparably linked. Submission to a false Jesus inevitably leads to twisted spirits and a perversion of the true gospel. Although we don't know the exact content of the false teachings Paul was opposing, it seems to have something to do with status enhancement and power, rather than proclaiming a humble, suffering Messiah. Paul's words offer a strong warning today, in which we hear the false gospel of a triumphant Christ, who offers health and wealth to those who seek him.

Reflection and discussion

- How can pastors, parents, mentors, and church communities express a "divine jealousy" for couples looking toward engagement and marriage?

- What are some false and deceptive teachings about marriage today?

- How can today's distorted understandings of marriage lead to confusion and mistakes for Christian spouses?

Prayer

Loving and jealous God, you have given us your Son, crucified and risen, your Spirit of truth, and the gospel of forgiveness and reconciliation. Keep me free from deception, faithful to the covenant, and devoted to Jesus Christ.

Husbands, love your wives, just as Christ loved the church and gave himself up for her, in order to make her holy by cleansing her with the washing of water by the word. EPH 5:25–26

Spousal Love in Christ

EPHESIANS 5:21–32 ²¹*Be subject to one another out of reverence for Christ.*
²²*Wives, be subject to your husbands as you are to the Lord.* ²³*For the husband is the head of the wife just as Christ is the head of the church, the body of which he is the Savior.* ²⁴*Just as the church is subject to Christ, so also wives ought to be, in everything, to their husbands.*
²⁵*Husbands, love your wives, just as Christ loved the church and gave himself up for her,* ²⁶*in order to make her holy by cleansing her with the washing of water by the word,* ²⁷*so as to present the church to himself in splendor, without a spot or wrinkle or anything of the kind—yes, so that she may be holy and without blemish.* ²⁸*In the same way, husbands should love their wives as they do their own bodies. He who loves his wife loves himself.* ²⁹*For no one ever hates his own body, but he nourishes and tenderly cares for it, just as Christ does for the church,* ³⁰*be-cause we are members of his body.* ³¹*"For this reason a man will leave his father and mother and be joined to his wife, and the two will become one flesh."* ³²*This is a great mystery, and I am applying it to Christ and the church.*

As the covenant of marriage was a common image used by the proph-ets to describe God's covenant with Israel, Paul deploys this meta-phor to describe the relationship of Jesus Christ with his church. Like Jesus when he taught on marriage, Paul reaches back to the original plan of God for man and woman expressed in Genesis: "For this reason a man will leave his father and mother and be joined to his wife, and the two will become one flesh" (verse 31). Christ's intimate "one flesh" unity with his church, which is expressed most fully in Eucharist, finds its most appropriate analogy in the "one flesh" communion of marital love.

Since marital love is the sacramental sign of God's love for his people and of Christ's love for his church, then marriage must accurately reflect the divine love. It must be faithful, permanent, self-giving, monogamous, indissoluble, generative, and fruitful. A married couple is a living sign for the whole community that God is loving and merciful, generous and self-giving, loyal and steadfast, and wonderfully creative.

The relationship within marriage upon which Paul draws his analogy is rooted in the cultural code of Greco-Roman society. The patriarch was the supervisor of his household, the head of his wife and children, who are required to obey him. However, Paul, while not overturning the norms of the culture, shows how marriage is transformed when understood as a sacramental image of Christ and his church. Instead of creating a relationship of male dominance, Paul tells husbands and wives, "Be subject to one another out of reverence for Christ" (verse 21). The responsibilities within marriage are mutual. Husbands and wives are to submit to each other, willingly responding to the needs of the other. Likewise, he tells husbands to love their wives in the way that Christ loves the church, completely submitting himself for the good of his spouse in self-sacrificial love. For Christian marriage, Christ is the example who determines the qualities of mutual submission, headship, respect, and love. Paul shows that for Christian marriage there is no place for authoritarianism, self-assertion, and self-centeredness.

The ritual bath, taken by the bride the morning of the wedding, was a necessary preparation for Jewish marriages. Paul says that Christ himself cleanses his church "with the washing of water by the word." It is a nuptial bath that not only purifies but also transforms the bride into perfect holiness and beauty (verses 26–27). The Torah teaches that a husband has three fundamental obligations to his wife: to provide her with food, clothing, and conjugal rights. In Paul's text, he describes the elegant wedding garment provided by Christ for his bride, and then he says that Christ "nourishes and tenderly cares" for his church (verse 29). Christ provides all this to the church, giving himself up for her, as an expression of his love.

Based on the incarnate love Paul experienced from Christ as the messianic bridegroom of his church, Paul set forth his exhortations to the married couples of his community. These early Christians recognized that their marriages were to be lived in the Lord and transformed by grace, a living sign reflecting the love of Christ for his church.

Reflection and discussion

- The ways that couples fail to love each other are often the ways we fail to love Christ. What are my most common failures in love?

- What can I learn from Paul's description of the husband-wife relationship in marriage?

- Christ clothes his church in baptism and feeds his church in Eucharist. How can receiving the sacraments as husband and wife strengthen and enrich a Christian marriage?

Prayer

Lord Jesus, loving spouse of your church, you call husbands and wives to reflect your love in Christian marriage. Help me to experience your spousal presence in my life, and give me the grace I need to be a visible sign of your love in the world.

In this is love, not that we loved God but that he loved us and sent his Son to be the atoning sacrifice for our sins. 1 JOHN 4:10

God's Love Casts Out Fear

1 JOHN 4:7–19 *⁷Beloved, let us love one another, because love is from God; everyone who loves is born of God and knows God. ⁸Whoever does not love does not know God, for God is love. ⁹God's love was revealed among us in this way: God sent his only Son into the world so that we might live through him. ¹⁰In this is love, not that we loved God but that he loved us and sent his Son to be the atoning sacrifice for our sins. ¹¹Beloved, since God loved us so much, we also ought to love one another. ¹²No one has ever seen God; if we love one another, God lives in us, and his love is perfected in us.*

¹³By this we know that we abide in him and he in us, because he has given us of his Spirit. ¹⁴And we have seen and do testify that the Father has sent his Son as the Savior of the world. ¹⁵God abides in those who confess that Jesus is the Son of God, and they abide in God. ¹⁶So we have known and believe the love that God has for us.

God is love, and those who abide in love abide in God, and God abides in them. ¹⁷Love has been perfected among us in this: that we may have boldness on the day of judgment, because as he is, so are we in this world. ¹⁸There is no fear in love, but perfect love casts out fear; for fear has to do with punishment, and whoever fears has not reached perfection in love. ¹⁹We love because he first loved us.

erhaps the greatest expression of who God is can be found here in John's climactic insight, "God is love" (verses 8, 16). After all the Bible has told us about God, and after all God has taught us about love, the insight of John expresses the very essence of God in this profoundly simple statement. To realize that God is love is to understand the reason for all the works of God throughout history. All that God does is a manifestation of this love. Love cannot exist in isolation, so all of creation is God's desire to express and share his very nature, which is love.

We experience something of the diffusive nature of love in our desire to give to other people. When we experience something good, we want to share it with others. When we gain new knowledge, we want to tell it to others. When we see something beautiful, we want others to see it too. Perhaps the best illustration of God's expansive love is the desire of a married couple to have a child. Their love for each other is so great it overflows their own lives into the creation of new life.

Since "love is from God," all acts of real love are reflections of God's nature. Whenever we love, we are experiencing something of the very life of God. Since we are made in God's image and likeness, we are made to express love. When we are loving, we are fulfilling what we were made to be.

The absoluteness of God's love comes to its fullest expression in sending his only Son into the world and, supremely, in his atoning sacrifice for our sins (verses 9–10). This is the definitive expression of love, the true standard of authentic love. The gift of God's only Son shows us that God's love for us is completely unrestrained. It also shows us that God's love is undeserved. God did not send the Son because we reached out in love, but because God reached out to reconcile us in our sinfulness. The initiative in loving is totally God's. Any love that we are able to experience is only because God has first reached out in love to us.

This love that God has shown us becomes our mandate to love in this same way: "Since God loved us so much, we also ought to love one another" (verse 11). Even though "no one has ever seen God" (John 1:18), God's presence can be felt and truly experienced at work within the world when we love one another. In fact, our loving becomes the means God uses to live in us and to continually perfect his love within us (verse 12).

We realize that our experiences of love are always incomplete. Our hearts are always unsettled, longing for fuller and deeper realizations of love. Even the most happily married couples sense a void in their love, a space in their hearts that cannot be filled by another. This yearning is a constant reminder that only the perfect experience of God can fill the deepest longings of our heart.

If we do not love, we shut ourselves up in a cocoon made of self-conscious-ness, suspicions, possessions, and fears. We build up defenses that keep us at a safe distance from the real world of living in union with other people. Becoming prisoners of our fears, we put up barriers that we think we need for our self-protection. But when we allow God to love us, we become less afraid, the cocoon of our defenses begins to break open, and we become more free and alive. We allow ourselves to be vulnerable in loving others.

This divine love working within us casts out fear, so that we have no reason to be afraid of God's judgment (verses 17–18). Whatever fear we may have simply indicates that our transformation in love is incomplete. As we allow God's love to complete its work in us, there is no more room for fear. We can have deep trust in God and great confidence in our eternal future. Our hearts expand with care and concern for others, becoming less self-centered and more other-centered. In this way, divine love is continually perfected within us.

Reflection and discussion

- How have I experienced the love of God breaking down my fears and enabling me to be more open to the world and more loving toward others?

- What have I realized about love through the twenty-one uses of the word in this passage?

- What are some ways in which married couples reflect divine love in the world?

- How does the message that "God is love" enlighten my understanding of the relationship between the Father, Son, and Holy Spirit, and of their relationship to us (verses 9–16)?

Prayer

Abiding God, since you are love itself, love is my origin, and love is my eternal goal. Cast out my fear as you perfect your love within me, and help me to know and believe in your love for me.

"Write this: Blessed are those who are invited to the marriage supper of the Lamb." REV 19:9

A Bride Adorned for Her Husband

REVELATION 19:4–9 *⁴And the twenty-four elders and the four living creatures fell down and worshiped God who is seated on the throne, saying,*
"Amen. Hallelujah!"
⁵And from the throne came a voice saying,
"Praise our God,
all you his servants,
and all who fear him,
small and great."
⁶Then I heard what seemed to be the voice of a great multitude, like the sound of many waters and like the sound of mighty thunderpeals, crying out,
"Hallelujah!
For the Lord our God
the Almighty reigns.
⁷Let us rejoice and exult
and give him the glory,
for the marriage of the Lamb has come,
and his bride has made herself ready;
⁸to her it has been granted to be clothed
with fine linen, bright and pure"—
for the fine linen is the righteous deeds of the saints.

⁹And the angel said to me, "Write this: Blessed are those who are invited to the marriage supper of the Lamb." And he said to me, "These are true words of God."

This vision of Revelation presents a hymn of worship in which the liturgy on earth joins with that in heaven. The assembly erupts in irrepressible joy because "the marriage of the Lamb has come, and his bride has made herself ready" (verse 7). The risen Lord is presented as the Lamb, an image from the Gospel of John in which Jesus is described as "the Lamb of God who takes away the sin of the world" (John 1:29, 36). Paul uses similar imagery when he calls Jesus the "paschal lamb" who has been sacrificed (1 Cor 5:7). The church is presented as his bride, an image with deep roots in the prophets and evangelists. Revelation expresses the reality that the slain Lamb has triumphed over evil, and God now reigns over creation. So the divine marriage of the Lamb and his bride has come, a timeless expression of the fullness of God's plan, the complete union of God and his people.

The boundaries separating the worshiping community in heaven and the one on earth blend together as they shout "Hallelujah"—a Hebrew word meaning "praise the Lord!"—in mutual confirmation that "the Lord our God the Almighty reigns" (verse 6). What better symbol of the new heavens and new earth than a wedding! Those who have rooted their lives in God's grace, who have followed the Lamb, will be united with Christ in an embrace of love that will bring life without end.

The writer proclaims that "his bride has made herself ready." This refers to the ritual process of preparing a bride for the wedding: the bath, anointing, and clothing in fine linen. Although Paul had said that Christ himself prepares the bride (Eph 5:26–27), Revelation suggests that the bride prepares herself, emphasizing the active responsibility of Christians in this preparation for final union with Christ. This preparation for the wedding is a continual process of both cleansing whatever elements make her unclean and putting on those qualities that make her beautiful for her spouse.

This active responsibility of the bride is qualified, however, with words suggesting the role of Christ: "To her it has been granted to be clothed with fine linen, bright and pure" (verse 8). Ultimately the wedding dress is a gift from her spouse. Christ offers his church the means and ability to attire herself as she does. The author decodes the symbol of the bright and pure linen dress by explaining that "the fine linen is the righteous deeds of the saints." The bride's attire is the sum of the saintly acts of the Christian community, the church's outward expression, the dazzling whiteness of her collective goodness, her intimate sharing in the risen life of Christ.

Revelation transports us out of the present trials to the end of the age. We are invited to envision ourselves as those who have received an invitation to the marriage of God and humanity: "Blessed are those who are invited to the marriage supper of the Lamb" (verse 9). But even more, we are invited to see ourselves as the bride, called to complete and faithful unity with our triumphant Lord.

Revelation was written to be read and heard in the eucharistic assembly of the churches. There Christ's past and future coming dissolve in the timeless moment of worship with the angels and saints. In its Eucharist, the church draws near to the Lamb who was slain, who lives now, and who will come again in glory. The church experiences in its worship the joys of eternal union with Christ in the feast of love that lasts forever.

Reflection and discussion

- Why is the slain and glorified Christ called "the Lamb"?

- Why does Revelation describe the new creation as the marriage of the Lamb and his bride?

- What elements of the Christian calling correspond to the bathing and clothing of the bride?

- How does the joyful worship of the Christian community lift me out of the present challenges of life and into my eternal life in the Lord?

- In what ways is the Christian Eucharist a celebration of the marriage supper of the Lamb?

Prayer

Lamb of God who takes away the sin of the world, how blessed are those called to share in your supper. I rejoice in the embrace of your love and the complete and faithful unity you desire to share with me.

Then one of the seven angels who had the seven bowls full of the seven last plagues came and said to me, "Come, I will show you the bride, the wife of the Lamb." REV 21:9

Presenting the Bride Who Longs for the Bridegroom

REVELATION 21:1–21 *¹Then I saw a new heaven and a new earth; for the first heaven and the first earth had passed away, and the sea was no more. ²And I saw the holy city, the new Jerusalem, coming down out of heaven from God, prepared as a bride adorned for her husband. ³And I heard a loud voice from the throne saying,*

"See, the home of God is among mortals.
He will dwell with them as their God;
they will be his peoples,
and God himself will be with them;
⁴he will wipe every tear from their eyes.
Death will be no more;
mourning and crying and pain will be no more,
for the first things have passed away."

⁵And the one who was seated on the throne said, "See, I am making all things new." Also he said, "Write this, for these words are trustworthy and true." ⁶Then he said to me, "It is done! I am the Alpha and the Omega, the beginning and the end. To the thirsty I will give water as a gift from the spring of the water of life. ⁷Those who conquer will inherit these things, and I will be their God and they will be my children. ⁸But as for the cowardly, the faithless, the polluted, the murderers, the fornicators, the sorcerers, the idolaters, and all liars, their place will be in the lake that burns with fire and sulfur, which is the second death."

⁹*Then one of the seven angels who had the seven bowls full of the seven last plagues came and said to me, "Come, I will show you the bride, the wife of the Lamb."* ¹⁰*And in the spirit he carried me away to a great, high mountain and showed me the holy city Jerusalem coming down out of heaven from God.* ¹¹*It has the glory of God and a radiance like a very rare jewel, like jasper, clear as crystal.* ¹²*It has a great, high wall with twelve gates, and at the gates twelve angels, and on the gates are inscribed the names of the twelve tribes of the Israelites;* ¹³*on the east three gates, on the north three gates, on the south three gates, and on the west three gates.* ¹⁴*And the wall of the city has twelve foundations, and on them are the twelve names of the twelve apostles of the Lamb.*

¹⁵*The angel who talked to me had a measuring rod of gold to measure the city and its gates and walls.* ¹⁶*The city lies foursquare, its length the same as its width; and he measured the city with his rod, fifteen hundred miles; its length and width and height are equal.* ¹⁷*He also measured its wall, one hundred forty-four cubits by human measurement, which the angel was using.* ¹⁸*The wall is built of jasper, while the city is pure gold, clear as glass.* ¹⁹*The foundations of the wall of the city are adorned with every jewel; the first was jasper, the second sapphire, the third agate, the fourth emerald,* ²⁰*the fifth onyx, the sixth carnelian, the seventh chrysolite, the eighth beryl, the ninth topaz, the tenth chrysoprase, the eleventh jacinth, the twelfth amethyst.* ²¹*And the twelve gates are twelve pearls, each of the gates is a single pearl, and the street of the city is pure gold, transparent as glass.*

The Bible begins with a poetic account of creation and the marriage of Adam and Eve, the archetypal couple representing the human ideal, and it ends with a beautiful description of creation perfected by its Creator and the eternal marriage of Jesus Christ and his bride. From Genesis to Revelation, the Bible is filled with expressions of God's spousal love for humanity. The gospels show us that the wedding of the Messiah and his bride has begun, yet it is not yet complete. Because preparing a home for his bride was the obligation of any Jewish groom, Jesus must ascend to prepare an eternal dwelling for his church. These final chapters of the Bible express the final unity of Christ and his bride, dwelling together forever.

Human language is incapable of expressing, and human imagination is incapable of perceiving, the perfection of God's kingdom. As Paul wrote, "What no eye has seen, nor ear heard, nor the human heart conceived, what God has prepared for those who love him" (1 Cor 2:9). Yet this does not hinder the writer from using a variety of images to evoke the goodness and splendor of God that permeates the resurrected life. It is like a new, perfected Jerusalem in which all can live, like the beauty of a bride prepared for her wedding (verse 2), as fresh and new as water from a spring (verse 6). Its wonder is due to the fact that God dwells with his people. God makes his home with humanity and cares for his people in all their needs: "[God] will wipe every tear from their eyes. Death will be no more; mourning and crying and pain will be no more" (21:4). God's people will finally experience the fullness of life, joy, and love.

Yet this fullness of God's will for creation is not reserved only for some distant future. God declares, "See, I am making all things new" (verse 5). The present tense indicates that God is already making things new right now. We have already begun to experience God's presence, divine comfort, and new life. To be sure, with the coming of Jesus, God has already begun a new creation in his Son and in all those who are united with him. Even if our experience of God's presence is often faint and fragmentary now, we can find consolation in this vision because we know that what we have experienced dimly will embrace us completely.

The climax of Revelation is the unveiling (*apokalypsis*, in Greek) of the bride. In Jewish weddings, the bride was unveiled to a song describing the bride's beauty in the sixth chapter of the Song of Songs. The lifting of the veil took place just prior to the consummation of the marriage in sexual union. In Revelation, the angel says, "Come, I will show you the bride, the wife of the Lamb" (verse 9). Going to a high mountain, the angel reveals "the holy city Jerusalem coming down out of heaven from God" (verse 10). The bride is the city of God, the new Jerusalem. Unlike the old Jerusalem of the prophets who was an unfaithful wife, this new Jerusalem has been cleansed and attired by her bridegroom.

This bride of the Lamb has twelve gates, inscribed with the names of the twelve tribes of Israel (verse 12). The walls of the city have twelve foundations, "and on them are the twelve names of the twelve apostles of the Lamb" (verse 14). And the bride is adorned with twelve kinds of jewels (verses 19–20), the same jewels worn by the high priest over his heart when entering the temple to make an offering to God (Exod 28:15–21, 29–30). Jesus the bridegroom is also the high priest of the new Jerusalem, the one who sees his church as a priceless treasure, who holds God's people upon his heart as he brings them into the house of God, where he will live with them in faithful love forever.

Reflection and discussion

• Why is the bride of the Lamb described as the perfected city of Jerusalem?

• God said, "See, I am making all things new." Why is this newness best expressed in symbols, metaphors, and images? How do I experience God's new creation today?

• God said, "I am the Alpha and the Omega, the beginning and the end." In what ways do the final sections of Revelation express the culmination of God's spousal love manifested since the beginning of Scripture?

Prayer

Alpha and Omega, the beginning and the end, you have created me and you recreate me with eternal life. Renew me in your Spirit so that I might experience the joys of eternal union with Christ in the wedding banquet that lasts forever.

SUGGESTIONS FOR FACILITATORS, GROUP SESSION 6

1. Welcome group members and make any final announcements or requests.

2. You may want to pray this prayer as a group:
   Lord Jesus, loving Spouse of your church, you call husbands and wives to reflect your love in Christian marriage, and you call all disciples to reflect the generosity and fidelity of your love. In the face of life's trials, sorrows, and suffering, assure us that nothing can separate us from that love. Cast out our fears as you perfect your love within us, and give us the grace we need to be visible signs of your love in the world. Renew us in your Spirit so that we might experience the joys of eternal union with you in the wedding banquet that lasts forever.

3. Ask one or more of the following questions:
   - How has this study of God's spousal love deepened your life in Christ?
   - In what way has this study challenged you the most?

4. Discuss lessons 25 through 30. Choose one or more of the questions for reflection and discussion from each lesson to discuss as a group.

5. Ask the group if they would like to study another in the Threshold Bible Study series. Discuss the topic and dates, and make a decision among those interested. Ask the group members to suggest people they would like to invite to participate in the next study series.

6. Ask the group to discuss the insights that stand out most from this study over the past six weeks.

7. Conclude by praying aloud the following prayer or another of your own choosing:
   Holy Spirit of the living God, you inspired the writers of the Scriptures and you have guided our study during these weeks. Continue to deepen our love for the word of God in the holy Scriptures and draw us more deeply into the heart of Jesus. Thank you for your merciful, gracious, steadfast, and faithful love.

Ordering Additional Studies

AVAILABLE TITLES IN THIS SERIES INCLUDE...

Advent Light

Angels of God

Divine Mercy

Eucharist

The Feasts of Judaism

The Holy Spirit and Spiritual Gifts

Jerusalem, the Holy City

Mysteries of the Rosary

The Names of Jesus

People of the Passion

Pilgrimage in the Footsteps of Jesus

The Resurrection and the Life

The Sacred Heart of Jesus

Stewardship of the Earth

The Tragic and Triumphant Cross

Jesus, the Messianic King
(Part 1): Matthew 1–16

Jesus, the Messianic King
(Part 2): Matthew 17–28

Jesus, the Word Made Flesh
(Part 1): John 1–10

Jesus, the Word Made Flesh
(Part 2): John 11–21

Jesus, the Suffering Servant
(Part 1): Mark 1–8

Jesus, the Suffering Servant
(Part 2): Mark 9–16

Jesus, the Compassionate Savior
(Part 1): Luke 1–11

Jesus, the Compassionate Savior
(Part 2): Luke 12–24

Church of the Holy Spirit (Part 1):
Acts of the Apostles 1–14

Church of the Holy Spirit (Part 2):
Acts of the Apostles 15–28

The Lamb and the Beasts:
The Book of Revelation

TO CHECK AVAILABILITY OR FOR A DESCRIPTION
OF EACH STUDY, VISIT OUR WEBSITE AT

**TWENTY-THIRD
PUBLICATIONS**

www.ThresholdBibleStudy.com
OR CALL US AT **1-800-321-0411**